CANADA
INSIDE OUT

How We See Ourselves,
How Others See Us

David Olive

Doubleday Canada Limited

Canadian Cataloguing in Publication Data

Olive, David, 1957–
  Canada inside out

ISBN 0-385-25611-6

1. National characteristics, Canadian—Humor. 2.
Canada—Public opinion—Humor. 3. Canada—Foreign
public opinion—Humor. 4. Canadian wit and humor
(English).* I. Title.

FC97.055 1996   971'.00207   C96-930586-9
F1021.2.055 1996

Jacket design by Avril Orloff
Text design by Heidy Lawrance Associates
Printed and bound in the USA

Published in Canada by
Doubleday Canada Limited
105 Bond Street
Toronto, Ontario
M5B 1Y3

*To my parents, Bonnie and Harold, the first to show me
why Canada matters.*

"Canada is the finest country in the world, Miss Cornelia."
"Nobody ever doubted that," said Miss Cornelia complacently.

Lucy Maud Montgomery, *Rainbow Valley*

CONTENTS

ACKNOWLEDGEMENTS

I wish to thank John Pearce and the staff of Doubleday Canada for their assistance in making this book possible. I would also like to cite, as a source of raw material and, more important, a great deal of inspiration, the work of previous compilers—most notably John Robert Colombo, master gatherer of Canadian quotations; and Greg Gatenby, editor of two volumes of writing by foreigners about Canada: *The Wild Is Always There* and *The Very Richness of That Past*. In place of a bibliography, I simply recommend two books that convey a profound understanding of the importance of what Canadians have achieved, Bruce Hutchison's *The Unknown Country: Canada and Her People* (1942), and his *The Struggle For The Border* (1955). Much history has been made and written about since those volumes appeared, but it continues along much the same noble lines.

PREFACE: WE OF LITTLE FAITH

I think it was just as they were singing like this: "*O—Can-a-da*,"
that word went round that the boat was sinking.

Stephen Leacock in *Sunshine Sketches of
a Little Town*, 1912

I did not learn how deeply flawed Canada was until, in my
early teens, I first took up the habit of reading a daily newspaper. Ostensibly a fount of good news, and easily the most
patriotic major paper in the country at that time, the *Toronto
Star* constantly fretted that its hometown was not keeping
up with the pace of civic modernization set by New York,
that our economy had almost completely slipped into the
hands of foreigners, and that we should feel ashamed that
our external-affairs polices were set in world capitals other
than our own. And it warned that we shouldn't flatter ourselves in thinking that much could be done about any of this.
In more chirpy moments, it trumpeted local virtues, once
asking, "Who says Canadians are boring?" Some thirty years
later, I still cringe at the abject humility that prompts such
a question.

In my neighbourhood, where we busied ourselves with

Centennial projects and gave rapt attention to stories our friends brought back from their first visits to Stanley Park and Fortress Louisbourg, and in our school, where we celebrated the day the Maple Leaf alone decorated each classroom, the Union Jacks having quietly been placed in storage —in that small world of my childhood, Canada was tops.

Only as I gradually was drawn into our larger national conversation, by way of newspapers, magazines, books and television documentaries, did I begin to learn that we were, it seemed, occupying one of the less favoured places in the sun. The negativism was, and is, incessant. Its object, no doubt, was to prod us to be better. But measuring ourselves against implausible standards of comparison—Massey Hall's fine, but it's nothing like Garnier's Opéra (well, what is?)— we invariably fell short. If the operating principle of most new nations, and of the U.S. to this day, is to assert superiority and then attempt to fill out a grand costume, Canada seemed to have turned this concept on its head. Even now, we begin by assuming our insignificance, and are only bemused, rarely allowing ourselves to be rah-rah delighted, when we outgrow our stunted expectations.

Defying limitations placed on us by daunting climate and geography, historical traditions that augur poorly for multiethnic, multilingual populations and for nations attempting sovereign coexistence with vastly more powerful neighbours, our underpopulated country has emerged in a scant half-dozen generations as an economic giant and a model of social progress with few if any equals in the world. Yet our preferred sense of inferiority attempts to deny that record, mocks and ignores it. Real limitations we have. But the only one that matters is a self-inflicted wound—this mythic invention of Canada as a second-best country.

Just listen to what we have to say for ourselves:

The climate, of course, is unforgiving. "This is a country," poet Alden Nowlan reminds us, "where a man can die simply from being outdoors." A *big* country—too big, in fact. "If some countries have too much history, we have too much geography," complained Mackenzie King, one of many prime ministers to assert that it was beyond his poor power to render such an unweildly space governable. Or for any of us to make ourselves at home in. "We are all immigrants to this place even if we were born here," says novelist Margaret Atwood. "The country is too big for anyone to inhabit completely, and in the parts unknown to us we move in fear, exiles and invaders."

Virtues we have, in abundance, but they are the wrong ones. "We Canadians are a worthy, thrifty people, perfectly safe and constituting no problem to the countries in control of our destinies," writes the distinguished historian A.R.M. Lower. "We are therefore uninteresting." We are boring, for want of boldness. "The Canadian is mildewed with caution," observed Marshall McLuhan, and this includes our regard for excellence, which merits only a tepid pursuit. "Canada is a country where everyone feels so much more comfortable with amateurs," writes journalist Barbara Amiel, who now lives mostly in London, and this explains why so many talented people have drifted away. As Eric Nicol puts it, "Some are born great, some achieve greatness, some have greatness thrust upon them, and some remained in Canada." Indeed, to know the full measure of success, one must at some point accept a job offer from abroad. "My generation of Canadians," editor and columnist Robert Fulford says, "grew up believing that if we were very good or very smart, or both, we would someday graduate from Canada." It follows that those of us who remain, held back in this remedial-school land, are not quick to applaud each other's achievements, and are generous only with criticism. This makes for a culture of resentment, shot through with pettiness. "These are Canadian lobsters, boys," goes the Maritimes story, and "as soon as one makes it to the top, the others will drag him down." Those who dare to be great risk censure, for we are a country "of smugness and sanctimony, tinged with envy and suspicion of success," says press lord Conrad Black. "Unless a person is a septuagenarian, a professional hockey player, or one variety or another of social worker, success is unbecoming, suspect and even un-Canadian."

In any case, the prospects of encountering success, becoming or otherwise, are severely limited. For we lack the necessary imagination: "Canada has produced no writer who is a classic in the sense of possessing a vision greater in kind than that of his readers," lamented literary scholar Northrop Frye. "Canadian culture," says novelist Barry Callaghan, who tries to be encouraging, "is at the very front of the second rank." Our commercial instincts are equally dull. "We invent nothing," as Archibald MacMechan has noted, and anything we might invent would likely languish for inattention. "If Canada invented the wheel," says technology expert Denzil Doyle, "it would drag it on a sled to be marketed in the United States." And why not, given our hostile climate for business? "If you have some money in Canada, why would you dig a foundation, put up a building, buy machines and cope with the bureaucratic environment," asks auto-parts czar Frank Stronach of Magna International, "when you can buy government bonds? No risk, no bureaucracy." It is no wonder, then, that our economy is foreign-owned. And having so eagerly sold our birthright, we have no cause to complain.

We are an unknown people; we do not even know ourselves. We relate not to this place, but to where we came from: "Everybody in this country," says novelist Hugh Hood, "has the psychology of a member of a minority group, and not a very important minority group either." Holding high the banner of reverse-chauvinism, we don't suffer patriots, not knowing the meaning of the word. "Canada is not an easy country for patriots; the word itself is all but lost in the language," says political commentator Dalton Camp. "Patriotism is an Americanism, a solid, substantial American virtue, with its legacy in the revolution that changed the sweep of history. It is a nothing word in Canada." Being so uncertain of ourselves, we cannot help being an awkward, apologetic presence on the world stage, answering to playwright John Gray's descripton of Canada as "the Woody Allen of nations." A nation which, even if it was blessed with more than a modicum of self-respect, could not defend itself from invasion. After all, true "independence requires the power, on our own, to hurt an aggressor," runs the absurd argument of essayist David Frum, who seems trapped in a nineteenth-century mindset when assessing the true destiny and worth of nations. "Until we acquire our own nuclear deterrent," he fears, "we will be wards of our enemies."

Lacking nuclear weapons, or even the will to learn the lyrics to *O Canada*, why don't we just give up, call it a day? Canada has a sordid history, after all: "It became a nation," *Maclean's* editor Ralph Allen said, "because of the vainglory of the English; because of the treachery of the French (who could have protected their colonists easily); because of the incompetence of the Americans (who were on the verge of capturing the country twice); and because of the enslavement and virtual extinction of the Hurons, Iroquois and Algonquins." How can we be proud of a country that began as an act of coercion, in which the real motive of 1867 was to perform the unfinished work of assimilaton that began with the 1759 Conquest? "Confederation," André d'Allemagne has complained, "is genocide without end," and Quebec nationalist Pierre Vallières recognizes the plot for what it is—"nothing more than a vast financial transaction carried out by the bourgeoise at the expense of the workers of the country, and more especially the workers of Quebec."

Dishonour behind us, uncertainty ahead—why go on? "We have no policies, no convictions and no future," prominent economist Dian Cohen has said. "The big question should be, Why don't we give the country to the Americans? They seem to want it so much more than we do." We need also to face up to the unpleasant facts of our mongrelized heritage. For we are not so much a nation as, in Mordecai Richler's words, "a holding tank filled with the disgruntled progeny of defeated peoples. French Canadians consumed by self-pity; the descendents of Scots who fled the Duke of Cumberland; Irish the famine; the Jews the Black Hundreds ... Most of us are still huddled tight to the border, looking into the candy store window, scared by the Americans on one side and the bush on the other."

To be sure, dismay was the reaction when Quebec Premier Lucien Bouchard famously said in 1996 that, "Canada is divisible because Canada is not a real country." But many others have given voice to the same belief for many, many years—and not just Quebec separatists.

Canada is not a real country because "the political destiny of our country seems to be involved in utter uncertainty and impenetrable obscurity" (educational reformer Egerton Ryerson in 1865). Because "Canadian nationality being a lost cause, the ultimate union of Canada and the United States appears now to be morally certain" (historian and journalist Goldwin Smith in 1878). Because "we French, we English, never lost our civil war, endure it still, a bloodless civil bore" (poet Earle Birney in 1962). Because "in every generation Canadians have had to rework the miracle of their political existence" (A.R.M. Lower in 1968). Because "there are no spectacular choices in a country like Canada" (Pierre Trudeau in 1972). Because "there's nothing easier in Canada than to unite most of Canada against part of Canada" (Joe Clark in 1991). Because "the idea of Canada—the animating principle which alone allows us to believe that this existence is the right one—has long since disappeared. Whatever was noble or true or even coherent about Canada as an idea was beaten out of it years ago" (*Globe and Mail* columnist Andrew Coyne in 1994). And most painfully because, as Robertson Davies replied when asked by fellow novelist Mavis Gallant why Canadians don't love our country the way Americans love theirs, Canada is "not a country you love. It's a country you worry about."

One aspect of our self-styled inferiority is our sense that foreigners show an interest in Canada only when we become, ever so briefly, a trouble spot. The narrow victory of national-unity forces in the 1995 Quebec vote on sovereignty prompted an outpouring of foreign commentary, most of it to the effect that Canada, regarded by many foreigner observers as the most nearly-perfect country in the world, was nuts to let itself break up—and that the world would be poorer for such an outcome. "If tolerant Canada cannot share power across a linguistic divide," wondered *The Financial Times* of London, "what hope is there for more bitterly riven societies?"

In truth, just as foreigners don't feel our attentive gaze on them, we fail to appreciate the degree to which our civic, cultural, scientific and economic achievements and short-comings are under more or less continual scrutiny among outside observers. That the assessments are so often favourable should not be unexpected, given that an occasional visitor does not have to live with, and may not even be knowledgeable about, a country's chronic or more subtle problems. What is unusual is that foreigners seem predisposed to like Canada —it is fixed in their imagination as a new, civil, industrially vigourous and scenically breathtaking place. While we have no difficulty identifying and dwelling upon our difficulties, outsiders seek out aspects of our life and land that they expect will favourably impress them, and appear seldom to be disappointed.

The land itself, of course, occupies a large portion of the world's interest in Canada. And it is a place of wonders. French explorer Samuel de Champlain insisted that "you could hardly hope to find a more beautiful country than Canada." Of the St. Lawrence River, John Burroughs, the American essayist, writes, "One of the two or three great water-courses is before you. No other river, I imagine, carries such a volume of pure cold water to sea ... it is a chain of Homeric sublimities from beginning to end." U.S. novelist Henry James finds perfection at Niagara Falls: "The genius who invented it was certainly the first author of the idea that order, proportion and symmetry are the conditions of perfect beauty." The Thousand Islands were, for Charles Dickens, "a picture fraught with uncommon interest and pleasure." Some of the pleasures are of a majestic order: Arthur Conan Doyle realized a childhood ambition in Western Canada, saying of a visit to the Rockies: "I have seen my dream mountains. Most boys never do."

Others have found subtler enchantments: B.C.'s coastal forests were "the richest, greenest, most verdant I had ever seen" for American author Zane Grey; while the Niagara Parkway struck Winston Churchill as the "prettiest Sunday afternoon drive in the world." Franklin Roosevelt found his "beloved island" and summer retreat in New Brunswick; and for Alexander Graham Bell, sometime resident of Nova Scotia, there was no place on earth to match the beauty of Cape Breton. "Canada is a place of infinite promise," said British economist John Maynard Keynes, in part because "the hills, lakes and forests make it a place of peace and repose of the mind, such as one never finds in the U.S.A."

Cities hold the highest claim on some hearts. Victoria, said James Douglas, Jr., "appears a perfect Eden," Walt Whitman thought Toronto "a lively and dashing place," and science fiction writer Ray Bradbury, a century later, would describe it as "the most perfect city in the Western Hemisphere." French writer Michel Tournier fell "in love with Vancouver instantly, this city where it rains all day long and then produces the most sublime sunsets. It's impossible to paint here! The intoxication of impotence! The canvas stays blank while you feast your eyes." For exuberance one turns to St. John's, "the most entertaining town in North America," says travel writer Jan Morris, "suggesting to me sometimes a primitive San Francisco, sometimes Bergen in Norway, occasionally China, and often Ireland of long ago." French writer Paul Blouet found a more real France on this continent than in Europe, observing that Quebec City, "more than three thousand miles from home, happy and thriving—[was] a feast for the eyes, a feast for the heart." Montreal is one of the esteemed Michelin Guide's favourite cities: "Built around an extinct volcano, [it] sits majestically on its island in the St. Lawrence ... there is great cultural vitality and a *joie de vivre* unknown elsewhere in North America."

Outsiders are struck by our bravery—"Whenever the Germans found the Canadian Corps coming into the line, they prepared for the worst," noted British Prime Minister David Lloyd George—and by our level-headedness. "The Canadians were truly objective," writes American novelist James Jones, who reported on Canadian peacekeepers in Vietnam. "They had done enough of this 'peacekeeping' work across the world by now that they seemed to have developed a tradition in their Army about how to handle it." They are an enterprising lot, or so thought Jean Monnet, founder of the European Economic Community, who worked in Western Canada in his youth: "For the first time I met a people whose job was not to manage what already existed, but to develop it without stint. No one thought about limits; no one knew where the frontier was." This pioneering spirit applies in academe, as well, where iconoclasts are plentiful, at least in the view of George Bernard Shaw, who, observing that Canada "made professors of men who were in the vanguard instead of among the stragglers and camp followers," wondered "whether I had not better end my days in Vancouver, if not Saskatoon." Canadians are devout—"I am afraid they made me feel ashamed of my own lack of reverence," said Zane Grey of Nova Scotians—and place high expectations on the future: "They're about the only ones left who still believe in it all, the Canadians," says mystery writer John le Carré.

What attracted le Carré initially was the vibrant artistic community he found here—"people with a tremendous cultural appetite and with a great intellectual reach." Foreign writers come to Canada to study and meet fellow writers because Canada, for many, is the future of writing. "Canadian literature is gradually building an imaginative map of the country," says novelist Salman Rushdie. "It's rather wonderful for the writer to be in a place where there is still a lot to be done." Canadian writers Michael Ondaatje, Josef Skvorecky and Rohinton Mistry are turning Canada into a focal point of a new multicultural era in publishing that has resulted in Toronto becoming, in the description of editor Sonny Mehta of New York publishing house Alfred A. Knopf, "the new literary centre of the northern hemisphere." What merits French couturier André Courrèges's admiration is the fact that "you are so practical. You dress for warmth and for function, and function of course is the basis of all good design." The focus is music for saxophonist Bill Clinton, who told the House of Commons that, "As a musician I must thank you especially for Oscar Peterson, a man I consider to be the greatest jazz pianist of our time."

But more than land, lakes, cities and the creative expression of its people, it is the founding ideal of Canada that provokes interest far beyond our borders. It is a country conceived not as the casting off of an oppressor in a nearby palace or faraway imperial capital, or in pursuit of commercial or geographic hegemony, or forged in the cauldron of ethnic purity, but as a deceptively simple *entente* among far-flung regions and people of diverse languages, customs and religions, pledged only to bend themselves collectively to the task of taming a raw land in a hostile climate, and beholden, perhaps overly so, to one golden ideal: civility in all things. This civility, which invites tolerance of the regionalism, social welfarism and cultural disunity that drives our complaints about our polity, is the very same gold standard of pluralism that makes foreigners so powerfully want Canada to succeed.

Among the first to grasp Canada's potential as an idyll of social tranquility, a few decades before it came into political existence, were fugitive slaves in the U.S. South. "I remember as a child," said Booker T. Washington, "hearing my parents and the older slaves speak of Canada with such tenderness and faith for what it would do for our race that I had no definite idea that it had any tangible visible place—I thought it an invisible ideal." But it was real, and in the disguised lyrics of folk songs by which slaves transmitted the details of escape routes to each other, "The word for Canada was heaven," recalled Martin Luther King, Jr. On becoming a country, the parliamentary institutions Canada adopted struck some observers as being more democratic than those to the south. "The representation of the American people at Washington is democratic, but the Government is autocratic," claimed French writer Blouet in 1891. "In Canada, both legislature and executive are democratic." In the twentieth century, the Washington, D.C.-based *New Republic* would complain that, but for the lack of a Canadian parliamentary system, a Watergate-wounded Richard Nixon could have been briskly dispatched from office in the space of two weeks. "Democracy is so new to those of us who live in a South American country," says Argentine author Jorge Luis Borges. "Canada: here there is freedom." The political climate is more temperate, as well. "You have a conservative tradition as well as a liberal tradition, and these supplement and complete and sustain each other," notes U.S. Senator Daniel Patrick Moynihan. "The United States lacks and has suffered for the absence of what could be called a conservative tradition. The people we call conservatives are really nothing more than rich anarchists." An egalitarian ideal is reflected by a bureaucracy much scorned at home, but thought by British novelist and ex-civil servant C.P. Snow to be "the finest civil service in the world today." The programs it administers are perceived as a bulwark of social reform. "It is the expectation of Canada's social system to look after the people who cannot take care of themselves," says U.S. novelist John Irving. "There is no such expectation in the United States [and] I do not think that Canada's social welfare system would prevail in the United States." Ralph Nader observes that "Time and again, in striving to improve consumer rights in the United States, my colleagues and I would make reference to a superior situation in Canada such as the provincial ombudsman, cheaper pharmaceutical prices, complete health-insurance coverage, and greater concern over acid rain."

Civility in the international arena is a Canadian hallmark. "The United Nations has come to expect in its debates to hear from Canada the voice of reason and enlightenment, rejecting the extreme of partisanship, seeking patiently the common ground for men of good will," said U.N. secretary-general Dag Hammarskjold. "The world is greatly indebted to Canada for the patient, skillful and unassuming work of her statesmen in many international contexts, including the United Nations," says Anglo-American diplomat Conor Cruise O'Brien. "Few countries can have attracted more genuine admiration, respect and liking, for their contribution to international affairs." Canada is a leading exporter of conciliation because, as Barbara Ward has noted, "Of all the middle powers, Canada has the greatest resources, the most central position, the finest web of contacts and influences and, relatively speaking, the highest proportion of experts, both bilingual and in each language, of any nation in the world." It has the makings, Ward felt, of becoming the world's first "international nation."

In the context of our current tenuous unity, historians remind us that certain New England states nearly broke from the Union after the defeat to Canada in the War of 1812, a conflict they did not support. And as the Civil War loomed, American novelist Nathaniel Hawthorne, a stout Northerner, asked a friend in England if the British crown might be persuaded to unite "Canada, New England and Nova Scotia. Those regions are almost homogeneous as regards manners and character and cannot long be kept apart, after we lose the counterbalance of our Southern States. For my part, I should be very glad to exchange the South for Canada."

We learn from such episodes that there is life after unity

crises, and are reminded that annexationist forces in the U.S. coveted Canada for a reason. "The policy which the United States actually pursues is the infatuated one of rejecting and spurning vigorous and ever-growing Canada, while seeking to establish feeble states out of decaying Spanish provinces," complained former U.S. secretary of state William Seward in 1857. Confederation was in part inspired as a means of thwarting such designs, but the envy continues. "There is something in the air here, or in Canadians, that makes the place more attractive than the United States," said American literary critic Edmund Wilson. "It must be like the Republic was some fifty years ago, before things took a turn for the worse." Explaining the motive for his 1985 book about Canada, *New York Times* correspondent Andrew H. Malcolm said, "It seemed to me that Canada, one of the world's best kept secrets, was an exciting place of new beginnings next door to an aging nation full of fear for its decay."

If we too have fears, mostly about our identity, Malcolm wonders why. "What's the matter with a Canadian culture, Canadian efficiency, and Canadian government consisting of pieces from all over assembled into unique forms?" Maybe this "identity crisis" of ours is a conspiracy, "an obsession more noticeable on campuses and in CBC television and radio stations than in the marketplace," as English author Malcolm Muggeridge mused. "Much of the apocalyptic rhetoric about the extinction of the Canadian identity," says American political commentator George Will, "comes from the Toronto intelligensia." And Canadians outside that charmed circle, Will says, "would be brave about the extinction of the intelligensia."

Probably we suffer from our imprecision, from having only a vague sense of who we are. Others are driven to an imagined appointment with greatness, while we must settle for a rendezvous with niceness. Which would suit some folks just fine. "It's too late for me to become Canadian, but I can understand the urge to be Canadian," says Anthony Burgess. And Jane Fonda says that "When I'm in Canada, I feel like this is what the world should be like."

"Warm-hearted, stable, fair to its many minorities, staunch in the cause of justice and democracy, Canada is one of the world's most highly respected countries," wrote Murray Sayle in a *New Yorker* essay following the latest Quebec referendum, arguing that Canada as it is currently constituted is a country worth believing in. Not bound by ethnic or linguistic ties, "Canada, by contrast, is a nation in the late-twentieth-century style: people of many backgrounds who share the same land and the same principles, and try to benefit from many cultures and creeds, in equality and mutual toleration."

Still we aren't convinced. "Canadians are perversely loath to face up to good news," says Canadian author and diplomat John W. Holmes. A favourite joke in the diplomatic rounds finds a Canadian abroad much exercised that his host has not yet said what he thinks of Canada. After much prodding, the host ventures a favourable opinion, only to receive a prompt rebuke: "Oh yeah, what would you know? You don't have to live there."

Many if not most of the Canadians quoted in this volume, expressing herein thoughts of a gloomy cast, have also spoken with affection, pride and urgent hope about their country and its future. At the close of hostilities in 1945, Bruce Hutchison marvelled that "We can hardly grasp the astounding fact that we have become suddenly one of the most powerful nations of the earth—an achievement, for our time, our population and our opportunity, without parallel in man's history." Accounting as we do for some 1/172,000,000ths of the world's population, and confronted with countless adversities, we can perhaps claim a pre-eminent achievement in nation-building. For it is true, as Joe Clark has noted, that "The Americans talk, with pride, of being the new world, the cradle of accomplishment. But we Canadians settled the harsher half of the North American continent. It was easier to build Virginia than to build Ontario." And most of us do cling resolutely to Canada's promise—it's in our blood. "Let the geniuses of easy virtue go southward; I know what they feel too well to blame them," Robertson Davies wrote. "But for some of us there is no choice: let Canada do what she will with us, we must stay." Much of what Canada has done is hugely agreeable, in the words of frequent critic Peter C. Newman, who allows that "the credo that has animated my work and my life is that Canda is the world's luckiest land." And this hour of our current adversity may yet mark us for greatness: "After feeling for more than a century that being Canadian was a journey rather than a destination," Newman wrote in his 1988 book *Sometimes a Great Nation: Will Canada Belong to the 21st Century?*, "we have arrived at last. We have attained a state of delicious grace which allows us to appreciate that what's important is not so much who we are but *that* we are—that sometimes a large nation can become a great one."

No assertion is made at home or abroad that Canada is a postcard-perfect land, and its reputation among foreigners reflects its faults as well as its blessings. Manhattan bond raters curse our fiscal folly, émigré entrepreneurs from Hong Kong are dismayed by a slower pace of business life, linguistic purists in France shudder at Quebec *joual*, Canada is significant to many Britons only according to the affection they hold for the second cousins they have lost to us.

Wyndham Lewis thought Canada to be "the most parochial nationette on earth"; and rock star Madonna, a victim of prudishness among constables who abruptly shut down one of her concerts, cursed "the fascist state of Toronto." *The Wall Street Journal*'s editorial board in 1995 conferred honorary Third World membership on Canada for its woeful over-indebtedness; and the branch-plant status of our industrial economy worries Lester Thurow: "Canadians have a good standard of living," Thurow has written, "but they can never have the best. The best jobs ... are back at headquarters, and that is somewhere else."

Yet it is the trivialization by some outsiders of Quebec's distinct society that is perhaps most painful to contemplate, given Quebec's acute importance to Canadians. Quebec has never commanded the degree of affection or respect in France that Quebec nationalists imagine, as was evident long ago with Voltaire's urgings that the royal court abandon the project of New France and accede to "my preference for Louisiana. I have never understood how one can prefer the most detestable country of the north, which we cannot preserve except by ruinous wars, and at the same time ignore the best climate in the world." In modern times, the tone of dismissiveness has only grown stronger. The author of Hachette's *Guide Bleu* for Canada, Alaska and Bermuda, wrote in 1967: "But do we care about knowing today that after Paris the city of Montreal is the largest French-speaking community in the world? Nostalgia for lost lands comes only with time." In 1960, a visiting delegation of Quebec cultural leaders expecting to find in Paris a warm familiarity with their concerns was taken aback when André Malraux, the French minister of culture, greeted them by saying that Charles de Gaulle, president of the Republic, had told him just yesterday, "Malraux, we have to take an interest in Quebec." In the early 1990s, Quebec premier Jacques Parizeau encountered the same indifference. After explaining his sovereignty mission to members of the French National Assembly, many of them wondered aloud why Quebec would want to transform itself into "an irrelevant micronation in the North American economy." In Britain, meanwhile, Prime Minister John Major has expressed his contempt for Scottish nationalists by equating their cause with the economic decline that bids for autonomy have brought about in Quebec, which he described in 1995 as "a high-tax, high-unemployment black spot with an uncertain political and economic future." French Canada is a second-rate place for American novelist Alice Colombo: "The French Canadians are *fous*, absolutely *fous*. Bombs, separatists. And worst of all is their atrocious way of speaking French." The U.S. magazine *Esquire* ridiculed the 1995 Quebec referendum: "*Egalite! Liberte! Stupidite!*"

Contrast that ignorance of the centrality of language rights, and of mutual accommodation as a defining vision of who we are, with Lester Pearson's succinct riposte to a reporter who asked how he explained the distinction between Canada and the U.S: "When Canadians are asked what difference there is between their country and the United States," Pearson said, "they should answer in French." It was a comment that assumed, correctly, a desire among most Canadians to make themselves at home in each of our two dominant cultural realities, and use our pride in that phenomenon as a form of national expression. To the extent that this has happened, Donald Creighton was right in observing that, "The French language has survived in North America for one reason only: because Canada has survived."

In the end, we are our only best friends, and our harshest critics. Strange that we should have witnessed in our own century the fast fade of the British Empire, the rise and fall of the East Asia Co-Prosperity Sphere, the Thousand Year Reich and the Soviet Union, the mourning by nativists in the U.S. for the lost glory of Pax Americana—and should be so merciless in our mockery of Wilfrid Laurier's predictive powers. The twentieth century has belonged to us, after all, and we have only begun to make a start. In nation-building, the race goes not to the swift but the stubborn, not to the sprinter but to those with the marathoner's strength of patient endurance. "Our souls are immortal, but our means are limited," Laurier admitted. "We constantly strive toward an ideal which we never attain. We dream of good, but we never realize the best."

Laurier dared to dream big. But are we more astonished at the breadth of his vision than he would be to know what we already have achieved? And when we stop dreaming of good, what then? Would Arthur Conan Doyle ever have gazed upon the Rockies had he not as a boy first conjured them in his mind? The question is not whether we are the equal of our dreams, but whether we have the courage to let them beckon us.

PART ONE

The Natural Inferiority of Canada

How We See Ourselves

THE LAND

[We] may be pardoned if we prefer London under the dominion of John Bull to Ottawa under the domination of Jack
Frost.

Nova Scotia statesman **Joseph Howe** in 1866

◆

[British Columbia is] an inhospitable country, a sea of sterile
mountains.

Central Canadian politician **Edward Blake** in
an 1874 Ontario speech

◆

Descriptions of our meadows, prairies and forests, with their
wealth of herbage and foliage, or artistic sketches of pretty
bits of lake scenery have their limitations as respects their
influence on a people. Great thoughts or deeds are not bred
by scenery.

John G. Bourinot, clerk of the House
of Commons, in *Our Intellectual
Strength and Weakness*, 1893

This is country of silent wind piling drift snow in Rocky
Mountains, trenches of quiet death, lonely desolation
George Bowering, "Far From The Shore"

❀

Too bad, that West of yours is so overgrown, lush—
unpaintable, too bad!
Painter **A. Y. Jackson**, letter to West Coast
painter Emily Carr

❀

If some countries have too much history, we have too much
geography.
Prime Minister **Mackenzie King** in 1936

❀

In land so bleak and bare
   a single plume of smoke
      is a scroll of history.
Poet **F. R. Scott**, "Mackenzie River"

❀

All we knew was that, however "young" the country might
be, the landscape seemed old and violent and sad.
Poet **Patrick Anderson** in 1957

❀

The Canadian Shield is fascinating country of enormous
wealth but there is too much of it. In Canada there is too
much of everything. Too much rock, too much prairie, too
much tundra, too much mountain, too much forest. Above
all, too much forest.
Novelist **Edward McCourt** in 1965

The coldest, darkest, and most barren regions ever inhabited by man.

Archaeologist **Robert McGee**, on
the Arctic Archipelago in Canada's
Northwest Territories

❋

If the national mental illness of the United States is megalomania, that of Canada is paranoid schizophrenia ...We are all immigrants to this place even if we were born here: the country is too big for anyone to inhabit completely, and in the parts unknown to us we move in fear, exiles and invaders. This country is something that must be chosen—it is so easy to leave—and if we do choose it we're still choosing a violent duality.

Novelist **Margaret Atwood** in 1970

❋

This is a country
where a man can die
　　　　　　simply from being
caught outside.

Poet **Alden Nowlan**, "Canadian
January Night," 1971

❋

But Canada has, for all practical purposes, no Atlantic seaboard ... To enter the United States is a matter of crossing an ocean; to enter Canada is a matter of being silently swallowed by an alien continent.

Literary philosopher **Northrop Frye** in 1971

You don't own the land. In winter, the elements own it, and in summer, the mosquitos.

Toronto business executive **Don Currie** in 1973

❀

More than most peoples, Canadians are prejudiced in favour of the ordinary: it is a function of our history, our climate and our geography. In a harsh land, we still honour all those pioneering virtues which impose restraint and engender mediocrity.

Authur **Charles Taylor** in 1977

❀

The winter half of North America.

Prime Minister **Joe Clark** on Canada

❀

My country's not a country, it's winter.

Quebec singer **Gilles Vigneault**

❀

Canada is the only Third World country with snow.

Montreal sports writer **Tim Burke** in 1983

❀

The challenging thing about the weather in Canada is that it's constantly changing—and you're always dressed for yesterday.

Writer and broadcaster **Adrienne Clarkson**
in 1988

This pattern of settlement sharply differentiated the Canadian experience from the American. [In the United States] the land was perceived as a garden as readily as wilderness, and it attracted far more settlers, and focused on European dreams,... The American occupation of an essentially welcoming land had the capacity to mold different peoples into a relatively homogenous culture as it spread them over an astonishing area. In Canada, all of this was checked by land's ineluctable niggardliness.

University of British Columbia historian
Cole Harris, cited in Andrew H. Malcolm's
1985 book, *The Canadians*

THE PEOPLE

French Canada is a relic of the historical past preserved by isolation, as Siberian mammoths are preserved in ice.
Historian and journalist **Goldwyn Smith** in 1878

✤

A refuge for people, who by reason of their indolence or lack of intelligence, could not succeed in other employment.
CANADA, *Report*, description of Canada, 1880

✤

O Child of Nations, giant-limbed
Who stand'st among the nations now
Undeeded, unadored, unhymned
With unanointed brow.
Poet **Charles G. D. Roberts** in 1882

✤

Another mistake which our leaders make is this—they seem to think the people are pure. It is a great mistake; they are as corrupt as the government that represents them at Ottawa.
Toronto *Globe* in 1882

Our souls are immortal, but our means are limited. We constantly strive toward an ideal which we never attain. We dream of good, but we never realize the best.

> Future prime minister **Wilfrid Laurier** in 1886

❦

I am done with the "Canadian Public" which consists of mere cattle.

> **Charles Mair**, member of the Canada First movement, in 1891

❦

How utterly destitute of all light and charm are the intellectual conditions of our people and the institutions of our public life! How barren! How barbarous! It is true that this is a new and struggling country, but one would think that the simplest impulse of patriotism, if it existed at all in our governing bodies, would suffice to provoke some attempt at remedy.

> Poet **Archibald Lampman** in 1892

❦

Our well-known Canadian laconicism is not always concealed wisdom, but a kind of dumbness, a frustration, a betweenness. We are continually on the verge of something but don't quite get there. We haven't discovered what we are or where we're going and therefore we haven't much to say.

> **Chester Duncan**

❦

Canada is too moral.

> Literary scholar **Douglas Bush** in 1922

In Britain, from an ancient society, there rise from time to time original thinkers who disturb the usual academic conservatism. As might have been expected, however, such are the conditions of the country, no arresting adventure in the realm of the spirit has yet been made in Canada.

Robert Falconer, president of the University of Toronto from 1907 to 1923, in 1927

❀

Our national soul has not grown beyond infancy.

Marius Barbeau in a 1928 speech on the importance of folk songs in building a national identity

❀

We are clever, imitative, but we seem to wait for someone else to show us the way, then we follow him, instead of carving out a path for ourselves. Just at the moment I can't think of a single creative work that can be credited to a Canadian... in art, architecture, literature, engineering or anything else. No doubt there are some, but nothing sticks out very strongly when measured by the old country, Europe or even the United States.

Artist **David Milne** in 1932

❀

You see before you a fairly complete cross section of the intelligensia of this city. I hope you are not too depressed.

Saturday Night editor **B. K. Sandwell**, introducing a visiting lecturer to a Toronto audience

The artistic cult of the North is, as a matter of fact, pure romanticism at its worst, and bears little relation to the real life of Canada. Far from seeking inspiration among the rocks and winds, the normal Canadian dreams of living in a big city where he can make his pile quickly and enjoy such urban luxuries as are familiar to him in the advertising columns of our national magazines.

Historian **Frank Underhill** in 1936

❦

If Canada does not often produce great artists, scientists, and professional men, it is not because the material is not amongst us, but because we do not know how to handle it. The characteristics of genius too often arouse our suspicion and distrust, whence it comes that our prophets are so often without honour in their own country. Perhaps if Canada had been a little different, Norman Bethune would not have died in China.

B. K. Sandwell in 1939

❦

Let any English-speaking Canadian sit down in his corner and divest himself of whatever is American in origin and impulse and culturally and intellectually he'll look like a half-skinned rabbit.

Arthur Phelps in 1941

❦

We Canadians are a worthy, thrifty people, perfectly safe and constituting no problem to the countries in control of our destinies: we are therefore uninteresting and what we write about is also, for the most part, uninteresting—except to ourselves.

Historian **A.R.M. Lower** in 1941

Canadians are very good second-bests.

A.R.M. Lower

✦

For we are young, my brothers, and full of doubt, and we have listened too long to timid men.

Journalist **Bruce Hutchison** in 1942

✦

They say we are more emphatically middling than any country west of Switzerland, and that boldness and experiment are far from our complacent thoughts.
Do you want audacity?
Let me tell you—
Any day in Montreal you may hear the guns crack at the noon-hour, as the police give chase to the bank robbers
Who are helping themselves to the wealth of the land like the

French and English before them, *coureur de bois* and fur trader rolled into one...

F. R. Scott, "Audacity"

✦

We remain the most inert, in the consciousness or use of our power, of women in nations the world over.

Ottawa mayor **Charlotte Whitton** in 1946

✦

Canada: a high school land frozen in its adolescence.

Poet **Earle Birney**

"I have given all I have to Canada—my love, my hate, and now my bitter indifference. But this raw, frostbitten place has worn me out and its raw frostbitten people have numbed my heart."
Novelist **Robertson Davies** in his play,
Fortune My Foe

❦

Canadians are a meek bunch; they'll take orders from anybody in uniform, including the milkman.
A.R.M. Lower in 1951

❦

We Canadians are a dull, unenterprising people. We have never enjoyed Prohibition, and never will. We take time out from business for a cup of tea and a crumpet, or to make love, or to have a snooze, or to do any other damn thing that appeals to us at the time.
Lionel Avard Forsyth, president of Montreal's
Dominion Steel & Coal Corp., in a 1950s
speech to an audience of New York bankers

❦

Canadians are perversely loath to face up to any good news.
Author and diplomat **John W. Holmes**

❦

Canada has no Jonathan Edwards, Jefferson, Franklin, or Tom Paine, no recognized spokesmen accepted as symbols of enlightenment, government, common sense, or the dignity of the common man. Canadian soil has not been friendly to the cult of the Great Man, the Tycoon perhaps, but not the Prophet.
Lorne Pierce, editor of the Ryerson Press
of Toronto, in 1960

A Canadian is someone who knows he is going somewhere, but isn't sure where.

Historian **W. L. Morton**

✦

"He doesn't want to talk about Canada,... There you have the Canadian dilemma in a sentence. Nobody wants to talk about Canada, not even us Canadians. You're right, Paddy. Canada is a bore."

Novelist **Brian Moore**, *The Luck of Ginger Coffey*, 1960

✦

A nation of losers.

Canada, according to **Robertson Davies**, who counted among the losers the defeated French colonists of New France, the American Loyalists who supported the losing side in the Revolutionary War, and the Canadians of Scottish blood who are largely descended from survivors of the battle of Culloden, in which the Scots met defeat by the English

✦

To Americans, Canadians are proof that the rule "Everything in moderation" can be carried to excess.

Eric Nicol

✦

We worry when you look hard at us, but we are also touchy about being overlooked.

Prime Minister **Lester Pearson**, address at Notre Dame University in 1963

Americans like to make money: Canadians like to audit it. I know of no country where accountants have a higher social and moral status.

Northrop Frye

❧

Discretion is surely one of the strongest and most negative virtues of the Canadian character … It plays a major part in robbing the scene of colour and vitality.

Hugh McPherson in 1965

❧

You have perhaps heard the story of the four students— British, French, American, Canadian—who were asked to write an essay on elephants. The British student entitled his essay "Elephants and the Empire." The French student called his "Love and the Elephant." The title of the American student's essay was "Bigger and Better Elephants," and the Canadian student called his "Elephants: A Federal or a Provincial Responsibility?"

Federal cabinet minister **Robert Winters** in 1966

❧

The leaders have been busy with the high mission of saving the northern half of the continent from Americanism, while thousands, millions of ordinary Canadians, French as well as English, have quietly emigrated and become American citizens.

Frank Underhill in 1966

❧

Does the history of mankind offer other examples of collective masochism as tenacious as the Catholic religion of Quebec?

Pierre Vallières in his 1968 political memoir
White Niggers of America

We're as soft as a kitten, we *pissous.*
> lyric from **Jean-Pierre Ferland**'s song *Pissou*
> (Coward), on Quebeckers' habit of accepting
> the lowest opinion of themselves

✦

I admire and covet not only American styles and achievements but also the American's generosity of spirit and willingness to take total responsibility for himself and his actions. A Canadian, by contrast, has been called someone who doesn't play for keeps.
> Historian **William Kilbourn** in 1968

✦

Everybody in this country has the psychology of a member of a minority group, and not a very important minority group either.
> Montreal novelist **Hugh Hood** in 1968

✦

One of Canada's greatest tragedies is that sober second thoughts so often prevail.
> *Globe and Mail* columnist **Richard J. Needham**
> in 1969

✦

Bananacanada.
> Novelist **Scott Symons** in 1969, referring to
> Canada's "banana republic" status in
> relation to the U.S.

Canadians do not like heroes, and so they do not have them.
Author **George Woodcock** in 1970

❦

I do not subscribe, pace too many embittered Canadian small talents, to the wildly self-flattering theory that there is an anti-Canadian cultural cabal common to London and New York. What I do believe is even more depressing. The sour truth is just about everybody outside of Canada finds us boring. Immensely boring.
Novelist **Mordecai Richler** in 1970

❦

Then, to repeat a favourite story of mine, there is the editor of a major New York publishing house who told me that one afternoon he and his associates compiled a list of twelve deserving but ineffably dull books with which to start a publishing firm that was bound to fail. Leading the list of unreadables was *Canada: Our Good Neighbour to the North.*
Mordecai Richler in 1970

❦

Canadians are, after all, simply romantics who lost the courage of their hopes.
Scott Symons in 1971

❦

Canada now, an imagined place
of strict decencies and the vast air,
where love might have prospered, and where
(as Dennis Lee would have it) we have failed.
Poet **David Helwig** in 1972

A gourmet, his greed notwithstanding, has a lot to offer
Canada. He is a seeker after excellence, and anyone in this
country who craves excellence in anything counterbalances
a Canadian weakness, the desire for an easy road, at the end
of which is mediocrity.

Sondra Gotlieb, food writer and wife of future
U.S. ambassador Allan Gotlieb, in 1972

♣

Canada demands a great deal from people and is not, as some
countries are, quick to offer in return a pleasant atmosphere
or easy kind of life. I mean, France demands an awful lot from
her people too, but France also offers gifts in the way of a
genial, pleasant sort of life and many amenities. Canada is
not really a place where you are encouraged to have large
spirtual adventures.

Robertson Davies in 1972

♣

I've noticed there's a sort of rueful pride in most voices when
they describe something as "typically Canadian." As if what
they were really saying was, "Well, we should have expected
as much." That's why our success at Expo was such a shock.
It wasn't *typical.* A typical Canadian success would have to
contain a basic absurdity, like a boat that wouldn't float, or a
prime minister with a lisp.

Pat Barclay in *The Victoria Times* in 1973

♣

Canada: The Retarded Giant on Your Doorstep

title for an article in a special edition of
National Lampoon in the 1970s that was largely
edited and written by Canadians

Although nearly all Canadian holidays are the same as the American ones, Canadian Thanksgiving is held a month early since Canadians don't have so much to be thankful for.
Journalist and *National Lampoon* contributor **Jack McIver** in 1973

❦

The Canadian is mildewed with caution.
Media philosopher **Marshall McLuhan**

❦

Canada is a country where everyone feels so much more comfortable with amateurs.
Journalist **Barbara Amiel** in 1975

❦

The trouble with Canadians—and if you've ever met one you will surely agree—is they suffer from an underdeveloped sense of the absurd.
Journalist **Geoffrey Stevens** in 1975

❦

Transcendental meditation, the prolonged effort to think of nothing, is a technique perfectly suitable for Canadians. They've been doing it now for almost a century.
Poet **Louis Dudek** in 1976

❦

Some are born great, some achieve greatness, some have greatness thrust upon them, and some remained in Canada.
Eric Nicol in 1977

The fact is, French Canada doesn't exist. French Canadians don't exist ... French Quebec is such a small, forgotten, culturally deprived, hyperactive and insecure community, no one would want to live there who doesn't have to, i.e. who isn't born into it. Lots of people are happy there, but always in spite of it, never because of it.
Le Devoir literary editor **Robert Scully** in 1977

✦

We peer so suspiciously at each other that we cannot see that we Canadians are standing on the mountaintop of human wealth, freedom and privilege.
Pierre Trudeau, former prime minister

✦

Canada is not an easy country for patriots; the word itself is all but lost in the language. Patriotism is an Americanism, a solid, substantial American virtue, with its legacy in the revolution that changed the sweep of history. It is a nothing word in Canada; in this country, the only word like it, in our vernacular, is loyalty. America has her patriots. Canada has the loyalists.
Journalist **Dalton Camp** in *Points of Departure*, 1979

✦

A lack of imagination, which, in turn, begets a lack of lusty voluptuousness. The inability to recognize that the proper conduct of a love affair requires diligence and practice, so that it can become an art form.
Michelle Bedard, author of *Canada in Bed*,
offering reasons why Canadian men make
good husbands but lousy lovers, in *The
Canadian Book of Sex and Adventure*, 1979

If bragging is a U.S. trait, self-denigration is 100 per cent Canadian.

Novelist **Jane Rule** in 1980

✿

Canadian society is deficient, not in respect for law but in respect for liberty.

Political scientist **Edgar Z. Friedenberg** in 1980

✿

We have no policies, no convictions and no future. The big question for this conference should be, Why don't we give the country to the Americans? They seem to want it so much more than we do.

Economist **Dian Cohen** in 1980

✿

We have tended too often to judge ourselves by imported values.

Journalist **Peter C. Newman**

✿

H.L. Mencken, the original American curmudgeon, once defined the columnist's role as that of comforting the afflicted, and afflicting the comfortable. This is difficult to achieve in a country such as Canada where the truly comfortable are imperturbable and the truly afflicted are inconsolable.

Dalton Camp in his 1981 essay collection
An Eclectic Eel

I have a certain clumsiness. Canadians, and I am one and proudly so, are forever apologizing for themselves. It's as though being Canadian is the original sin.

Actor **Donald Sutherland** in 1981

❧

In this country you can say what you like because no one will listen to you anyway.

Margaret Atwood in *True Stories*, a 1981 selection of her poetry

❧

Americans say, "We have nothing to fear but fear itself." A Canadian says, "Things are going to get a whole lot worse before they go bad."

From an early 1980s **Royal Canadian Air Force** sketch

❧

Americans cannot conceive of losing unless there's a conspiracy somewhere. Canadians, constrained by climate, distance and history, see no reason to expect victory.

Historian **J. M. S. Careless**

❧

Not bad for a Canadian, eh?

Steve Podborski in 1982, on winning the World Cup downhill skiing championship at Aspen, Colo.

We are not good with our heroes, we Canadians. Starved for figures of national interest, we, or our media, seek out anyone who shows a flicker of fame, and shove them on the nearest available pedestal. We leave them up there for a while, and then we begin to throw things at them.

Writer and broadcaster **Peter Gzowski** in 1981

❦

This being a small country, everybody's an insider. Everybody knows somebody who knows how flawed some famous person really is. And, failing that, virtue can be its own punishment, as in: "Wayne Gretzky? He's just ... well, he's just too perfect."

Journalist **Charles Gordon** in the early 1980s

❦

[Canadians are among the world's most] negative, parochial and balkanized people.

Canadian diplomat **Bruce Rankin**

❦

[Canada is] a kind of Woody Allen of nations.

Writer and broadcaster **John Gray** on Canada's awkward presence on the world stage

❦

Canada is over one hundred years old, and by now you'd think we would have come up with a national dish—something we could call our own, so we don't have to borrow hot dogs on July 1 or turkey on Thanksgiving.

Food writer **Cynthia Wine** in 1985

A few years ago, while visiting Mr. Galbraith at his farm in northern Vermont, I asked him why he had left Canada in the first place. "Well," was the drawled reply, "I was brought up in Southwestern Ontario, where we were taught that Canadian patriotism should not withstand anything more than a $5-a-month wage differential. Any more than that, and you went to Detroit."

Peter C. Newman in 1985, recalling an exchange
with economist John Kenneth Galbraith,
a native of Iona Station, Ont.

❀

When a nation's elite is less than three generations removed from steerage, it can't afford too many pretentions.

Peter C. Newman

❀

You can always tell a Canadian by the fact that when he walks into a room, he automatically chooses to sit in the most uncomfortable chair. It's part of our genetic affinity for discomfort and self-denial, which has formed the Canadian character as clearly as our geography.

Peter C. Newman in 1985

❀

A Canadian will work, or fight, or give money to philanthropic causes readily enough, but he will not think if he can possibly, at whatever cost, get someone else to do it for him. The Canadian is, in intellectual matters, a slob. There is a reason for this surrender. Good works are cheap in comparison with the solitary psychological hard work.

Robertson Davies in 1987

Canadians have traditionally prided themselves on the fact that after the turn of the nineteenth century there were relatively few armed confrontations between white and red men —certainly nothing on the scale of the Indian wars fought by the U.S. Cavalry. But this difference does not justify the smug assumption that white men north of the 49th parallel treated the native population with compassion and respect. On the contrary, the unrestrained use of liquor in the Canadian fur trade ranks as one of history's more malevolent crimes against humanity.

Peter C. Newman in 1987

✤

It is a sad fact that Canadians do not use the English language proudly or considerately. Sometimes I am driven to reflect that if there is a way to mispronounce or misuse a word, Canada will surely find it.

Robertson Davies in 1987

✤

Contrary to the fears of nationalists, baseball has not shrouded or in any way diminished [Canada's] national distinctiveness: even with all-American players, the Toronto Blue Jays managed to show the world that they too know how to win until it counts.

Journalist **John Fraser** in 1988

✤

We too often tend to apologize for drawing to someone's attention that they are standing on our feet.

Federal fisheries minister **Brian Tobin** in 1994,
on the previous Mulroney government's reluctance to confront the U.S. on overfishing of
the East Coast cod stocks

He told the story of the Maritime fisherman carrying a pail of lobsters up from the wharf. Another fisherman warns him that the lobsters might escape because there's no lid on the pail. "Oh, no," says the first fisherman. "These are Canadian lobsters, boys. As soon as one makes it to the top, the others will drag him down."

Toronto Star account of a speech by
Canadian diplomat **Derek Burney** in 1989

🍁

[*The Globe and Mail*] expresses so faithfully the English-Canadian characteristic I have often decried in this and other places, of smugness and sanctimony, tinged with envy and suspicion of success. Unless a person is a septuagenarian, a professional hockey player, or one variety or another of social worker, success is unbecoming, suspect, and even un-Canadian.

Writer and newspaper magnate **Conrad Black**
in the late 1980s

🍁

It could be we have this distaste for talking tall, for strutting around and really making a thing about the military.

Victor Suthren, director of the Canadian War
Museum, in 1995, bemoaning the Ottawa
institution's chronic underfunding, and offering the explanation that, "Maybe it's the fact
that Canada is not a nation that wants to
focus on its military history, even though
we're very good at being military
when we have to be."

Memory is a selective thing, and grievances are seldom forgotten. Whatever form Quebec takes, the impetus will come
not from a rational present, but an emotional past.

> **Stephen Godfrey**, Quebec arts correspondent in
> 1991, who recalled that the complete version
> of Quebec architect Eugène Taché's motto for
> Quebec, officially adopted in 1883, is,
> "I remember that born under the [French
> *fleur de*] *lys*, I grow under the [English]
> rose." Raising this matter with Jean Dorion,
> president of the St. Jean Baptiste Society,
> Godfrey was told that the motto is rendered
> only as "*Je me souviens*" today because
> Quebec prefers, Dorion says, to forget "cer-
> tain parts of history that are less pertinent."

❋

Canadians will complain for a few minutes, and then they'll
roll over.

> Liberal MP **Dennis Mills** in 1995, when asked
> about the likely impact of an expected hike
> in income taxes

❋

We like our heroes covered in humility and we take umbrage
when they presume to crown themselves. This is not solely
a Canadian trait, but in our own spitefully egalitarian way we
have made self-levelling something of an obsession.

> **Grant McCracken**, an anthropologist at the Royal
> Ontario Museum, in 1995

Canada has no national religion. Neither have we any national morality, nor a national attitude towards such concepts as work, profit, family structure, or the proper use of leisure. In all these and a thousand other areas, we are "pluralist" in our outlook.

The fact a person is Canadian will tell you nothing of what he assumes to be right or wrong in any of these areas. Notice there's a principle at work here: the wider the "pluralism" of any society the less the members of that society have in common. Every advance of "pluralism" is an advance of negativism. The totally "pluralistic" society would not be a society at all.

Ted Byfield, founder of *Alberta Report*
magazine, in 1995

✦

The last week has excited all the envious, whining, righteous, self-centred jealousies, grievances and insecurities that hold such a place of honour in this nation of sumkeepers. If there is one reason alone to avoid constitutional issues, it is to save the embarrassment of every wounded "people" lining up to wail about their humiliation and degradation compared with fellow citizens.

a 1995 *Globe and Mail* editorial commenting on
the frosty reception to Prime Minister Jean
Chrétien's recent proposals for constitutional
reforms, which by granting vetoes to certain
provinces only alienated those not to
receive one

I sometimes think a Canadian's idea of heaven is an eternal panel discussion.

Former federal cabinet minister **Marc Lalonde**,
on the interminable constitutional debate

♣

We have often defined ourselves as not being Americans. We lack their gift for mythology and instead of rallying around the image of Johnny Canuck or Lester Pearson, we see ourselves as quieter, less parochial, more peaceful than our neighbours. The act of defining oneself by a negative is the easiest and most attractive method. We identify the worst traits in others and note that while we aren't perfect, at least we don't have race riots or food shortages or drive-by shootings, etc., although we are making headway in all of those areas.

Journalist **Don Gillmor** in 1996

♣

Prime Minister Jean Chrétien has been proclaiming Canada the best country in the world on the basis of a United Nations study. That is not exactly what the U.N.'s 1994 Human Development Report has to say ...

The report finds that all countries with the required data treat women worse than men. When adjusted for gender disparity, the Human Development Index ranks Canada only eighth among the top 17—not much to write home about— with the Scandinavian countries and France heading the list ... When the HDI is adjusted for disparities between the income share of the bottom 20 per cent of the population and that of the top 20 per cent, Canada is again no better than eighth.

Charles Castonguay, associate professor
of economics at the University of
Ottawa, in 1995

The United Nations rates Canada one of the world's most desirable places to live, and so for many it is. But it has become, and probably always has been, a plain vanilla country. It hasn't the extremes of American life, neither the desperate, crime-addicted urban underclass that is slowly shrinking but still very evident in the U.S., nor the tremendous effervescence of talent and creativity that takes that country constantly forward to leadership in nearly every field ... [Canada] is undoubtedly a comfortable country, but we must face the fact that it is not particularly distinctive, creative, original or self-assured.

Conrad Black in 1995

✤

Resentment of big profits reveals a typically Canadian fear of success and ignorance of how business works. Are we secretly wishing all our banks were unprofitable?

Peter Ladner, publisher of *Business in Vancouver*, in 1996, on widespread criticism of Canada's Big Six banks after they reported record 1995 profits

✤

Whenever I'm away from Canada the thing I miss most is the apathy.

Toronto artist and social activist **Mendelson Joe**

CITY LIFE

Canadian cities are seldom marked by great architectural or other distinction which could attract a wide allegiance. The sky over Ottawa or Toronto or Montreal is still singularly unstained by any transcendent work of human genius.

Literary critic **E. K. Brown** in 1958

✦

The Quebec urban area has a soul—the Old City is a powerful spiritual force—but no heart. There is no engine pumping blood through the body, no energy which gives common purpose and will. It means there is an emptiness to the place, as though it is not complete as a city.

John Sewell, urban-affairs writer and former Toronto mayor, in 1986

✦

Montreal
The only city in the world where the sun sets in the North!
City entirely surrounded by sewers,
    one of which provides the drinking water.

Louis Dudek, "O Montreal"

Montreal is only a stop on the way from Belgium to Kentucky.
Jacques Ferron in 1972

❧

Montreal, my Montreal has become a city where you awaken each morning to count your losses.
Novelist **Mordecai Richler** in 1979

❧

The fabric of Canadian cities leans to architectural polyester. Most of our conspicuous buildings are mediocre copies of decent copies of foreign originals. The latest threat is sophomoric post-modernism, emerging most lamentably in Montreal. One need only gaze on urban Canada to see that we need more design literacy in place and in print.
Journalist **William Thorsell** in 1987

❧

The ugliest town in Quebec ... the ugliest city I have seen in the world.
Bloc Quebecois MP **Suzanne Tremblay**
in 1995, blaming Hull's unsightliness
on federal buildings erected by the
government across the river in Ottawa

❧

Ottawa is not a handsome city and does not appear destined to become one either.
Wilfrid Laurier

❧

The best thing about Ottawa is the train to Montreal.
Attributed to federal cabinet minister
Jean Marchand in the 1960s

Ottawa is a sub-arctic lumber-village converted by royal mandate into a political cockpit.

Goldwin Smith, on Queen Victoria's 1857 selection of Bytown, later Ottawa, as the capital of the province of Canada

❦

My Centennial project is to try to love Toronto.

Conservative Party leader **Robert Stanfield** in 1967

❦

Commiting suicide in Toronto is redundant.

Popular T-shirt at a **Rhinoceros Party** convention in Toronto in 1981

❦

In the 1950s, Toronto was just a large outdoor Woolworth's.

Journalist **Stephen Williams** in 1981

❦

Toronto is just Cleveland in rhinestone drag. The city is drowning in its own pretensions ... I don't find much public spirit in Toronto—people are too busy acquiring things for themselves.

Toronto art critic **John Bentley Mays** in 1989

❦

Underneath the flourish and ostentation is the old city, street after street of thick red brick houses, with their front porch pillars like the off-white stems of toadstools and their watchful, calculating windows. Malicious, grudging, vindictive, implacable.

Margaret Atwood on Toronto, in *Cat's Eye*

Cheaper airfares to New York.
> Artist **Charlie Pachter**, when asked to suggest
> how Toronto could be improved

❦

As a Canadian, I wish I could sit here, hand over heart and tell you otherwise. But the fact is, London is more interesting than Toronto. It's an endless sequence of sumptuous lunches and dinners with terribly interesting people from all over the world.
> **Conrad Black**, explaining his 1989 decision
> to trade Toronto for London as his
> principal residence

❦

So far as Winnipeg is concerned it is a discouraging place and always was, but I would not fret about it. I think it will come around all right. If it does not we can always have the satisfaction of consigning it to a warmer place.
> **Clifford Sifton**, Laurier government cabinet
> minister, in 1899

❦

Boy Meets Girl in Winnipeg and Who Cares?
> Essay title, novelist **Hugh MacLennan**, 1960

❦

You could live in Winnipeg a thousand years and not meet Ringo, Paul McCartney and Bob Dylan.
> Winnipeg-born rock singer **Burton Cummings**
> of The Guess Who, in 1977

❦

If You're So Good, What Are You Doing in Saskatoon?
> Title for popular Prairie drama of the
> early 1980s

No cities with the possible exception of Sodom and Gomorrah have ever been founded in less congenial physical surroundings than Regina, Queen City of Saskatchewan.

Novelist **Edward McCourt** in 1968

❀

Edmonton, like acne, is to be endured.

Mordecai Richler in 1976

❀

Edmontonians look down on Calgary as uncultured; Calgarians look northwards at Edmonton and dismiss it as "Siberia with government jobs."

Journalist **Richard Gwyn** in 1978

❀

Edmonton and Calgary have always suffered debilitating competition for population from Vancouver, which is at once so seductive and so available. The problem is not so much the brain drain itself as the soporific effect Vancouver has on the minds that succumb to its lure. Education goes a-wasting and career commitments falter. In such a setting, you don't have to *do*, to make a mark; it's enough to *be*. Vancouver is not just flower children gone to seed; it is saplings gone to bonsai. Its natural beauty uncontested, Vancouver is less than meets the eye.

William Thorsell in 1989

❀

Edmonton isn't exactly the end of the world, but you can see it from there.

Calgary mayor **Ralph Klein**

Vancouver is the suicide capital of the country. You keep going
west until you run out. You come to the edge. Then you fall off.

Margaret Atwood in *Cat's Eye*

*

The day I realized that Vancouver is a resort more than a city,
everything seemed to fall into place. You ask most people the
best thing about Vancouver, and they say it's the ability to get
away from it: to the mountains, the sea, the parks. This is not
a recipe for a throbbing urban environment.

Stephen Godfrey

*

Victorians will hate me, but their lovely city is simply a swirl
of bureaucratic bath water which all involved in government
constantly drink.

Vancouver radio commentator and former
B.C. legislator **Rafe Mair** in 1996, on why newly
sworn in Premier Glen Clark was spending so
much time away from the B.C. capital

ARTS AND ACADEME

Canada, or rather be it said Ontario, cooped up as it is and severed from the great literary and publishing centres, is not a field in which literary distinction is to be earned.

Goldwin Smith

❋

M. M. Garneau and Ferland have already, it is true, supplied a granite base for our literary edifice; but if one bird does not make a spring, two books do not constitute a literature ... The cause of this inferiority lies not in the rarity of men of talent, but in the disastrous environment provided for the writer by the indifference of a population which has as yet no taste for letters, at least for works produced by native sons.

Poet **Octave Cremazie** in 1867

❋

A Canadian book is sure, with the stigma of a colonial imprimatur upon it, not to circulate beyond the confines of the Dominion; and, therefore, when a Canadian writes a meritorious book ... he seeks a publisher abroad.

James Douglas Jr. in 1875

The more I reflect on the destiny of Canadian literature, the less chance I find for its leaving a mark in history ... Say or do what we will, we will always remain only a simple colony from the literary point of view, and even if Canada became an independent country and made her flag shine in the sun of nations, we should remain nonetheless simple literary colonials.

Octave Cremazie in 1867

❀

The bald truth is that Canada has the money, but would rather spend it on whiskey than on books.

Robert Barr in *Canadian Magazine* in 1899

❀

Were it not for the kindly offices of a very few interested people who impress the government with the necessity of providing sustenance to Canadian art by the occasional purchase of a picture from one of the annual shows, Canadian art would inevitably go under, or succumb to the popular forms of picture-taking, usually known as "pot-boilers."

Painter **Arthur Lismer** in 1920

❀

I remember an old lady who had a house full of second-rate European paintings saying, "It's bad enough to have to live in this country without having pictures of it in your home."

Painter **A. Y. Jackson**

❀

The salvation of Canadian literature would be a nation-wide attack of writer's cramp lasting at least a decade.

Douglas Bush in 1926

I find writing about the Canadian theatre or drama depressingly like discussing the art of dinghy sailing among the Bedouins. There is so little to be said on the subject save to point out why there is none.

> Playwright, journalist and historian
> **Merrill Denison** in 1929

❅

There is no spiritual gratification to be found in the sale of any book, no matter what kind of tripe, in Canada, no more than there is in the sale of a package of tea ... Canadians do buy books: the trouble is that there is not much sense of adventure in reading in our people: they go for the books that have a big sale in other countries.

> Novelist **Morley Callaghan** in 1939

❅

What is the market for the Canadian song writer? The answer is, almost none whatever.

> Toronto music publisher **Gordon V. Thompson**
> in 1943

❅

True comedy can be as serious as tragedy. A hundred grand plays are waiting for Canadians who will write them. But if there were a great Canadian play, would Canadians bother to stage it? ... Cover it up, good friends; cover it decently up with Canadian dust and let it lie. Some day the Americans or English will do it and tell us not to be ashamed and then, having their word for it, we will tardily take the duster and disinter a work once made in Canada.

> Playwright **John Coulter** in 1947

I left to seek my fortune in the United States in the years when it was possible to make a fortune.

Thomas B. Costain in 1951. The Brantford, Ontario-born Costain, former editor of *Maclean's*, went on to become a popular historical novelist in the U.S.

❦

What is really lacking is not Canadian criticism in any sense of the term but an audience for it ... Canadians do not care what other Canadians think.

E. K. Brown in 1951

❦

The wit of a graduate student is like champagne—Canadian champagne.

Robertson Davies

❦

No wonder our face looks blank to others. Even in films a Canadian to date has been either a half-breed trapper or a Mountie, or a contrivance for casting an Englishman in a Hollywood picture or an American in an English one.

Playwright and arts commentator
Mavor Moore in 1958

❦

Despite all the work we did in Toronto, and the hopes we had for it, there's really no more reason for Toronto to have a movie industry than Cleveland.

Sidney Furie, CBC-TV alumnus and director of *The Ipcress File*, in 1965

Contemplating the arts in Canada at the moment is (as Kingsley Amis has observed in another context) like listening to Mozart while suffering from toothache. There is a most agreeable background distorted by sensations of acute discomfort. The background is created by our artists and the organizations which employ them. The latter continue to grow in size and scope, and sometimes in stature. The discomfort is caused by a lack of funds adequate to maintain even a reasonable rate of growth.

Arts administrator **Peter M. Dwyer** in 1964

✤

In spite of what they'll say in the commissions on culture and the proliferating expositions and festivals and aids-in-grant to anybody who knows anybody else, the only true Canadian invention is a game called hockey.

Journalist **Ralph Allen** in 1965

✤

Canada has produced no writer who is a classic in the sense of possessing a vision greater in kind than that of his readers … There is no Canadian writer of whom we can say what we can say of the world's many major writers, that their readers can grow up inside their work without ever being aware of a circumference.

Northrop Frye in 1965

✤

We had to leave to be recognized. It was an anomaly. If we stayed, we were nobodies. If we went away and became successes, we were resented.

Melfort, Saskatchewan-born
actor **Arthur Hill**

There is no future for an actress in Canada. The Meccas are elsewhere.

> Toronto-born actress **Tony Robins**, a star in
> London's West End, in 1968

◆

This country [of Quebec] has said nothing, written nothing. It has not produced a fairy tale nor an epic to express, with all the artifices of invention, its destiny as conquered; my country remains and will long remain in sub-literature and sub-history.

> **Hubert Aquin** in his 1968 novel *Trou*
> *de memoire*

◆

I'm invited to do a command performance for the Queen in England. President Nixon has asked that I do a concert at the White House. But I don't get any requests from Trudeau. It sometimes seems pretty hopeless getting through to Canadians that yes, we Canadian artists do exist.

> Jazz pianist **Oscar Peterson** in 1969

◆

Canadian science has grown to resemble in some ways the Canadian Armed Forces. Recent reports indicate that for every private in the army there are four of higher rank. Now it appears that for every working scientist there are four persons spending their time deciding how and where and when he should work.

> Nobel laureate scientist **Gerhard Herzberg**
> in 1971

There's something about this country that allows exceptional films to be made only by accident. The talent and resources of this country are unlimited, and it's rather sad that these talents, over and over again, are wasted and wither up.

Film director **Peter Pearson** in 1971

✦

In Britain, you don't find special little book departments labelled "Britannia." In Sweden, no set of shelves labelled "Swedenia." We have a long way to go yet.

Publisher **James Lorimer** in 1972

✦

If Canada ceases to exist it is more likely to be death by hypnosis than by foreign investment. The vitality of the American media, from NBC to *Penthouse*, is such that Canadians are losing consciousness of themselves ... We are in danger of becoming a zombie nation, our physical structure intact but our souls and minds gone abroad. Having gloriously resisted with our loyal muskets the Yankee invader on the slopes of Quebec and Queenston, Canada may well be conquered by American television. That's a hell of a way to die.

John W. Holmes in 1974

✦

Canada is in the absurd position of having created—and of nurturing—a broadcasting system which would disappear if, by some chance, the San Andreas Fault became active and Hollywood floated out to sea.

Communications expert **Norman Spector** in 1976

It should be possible to turn on one's television set and know what country one is in. One would almost never be in doubt in the United States; one is frequently in doubt in Canada.

Media critic **Morris Wolfe** in 1974

❦

Nor have we, I'm afraid, any architectural masterworks—no Parthenons, no St. Paul's Cathedrals—nor any architectural geniuses. Canadians do not cultivate genius, for by and large they have never been hero-worshippers and the "star system" is not part of our culture. Perhaps our most fine and original Canadian design is the grain elevator; spare, clean-lined, candid about its function. Le Corbusier was very excited about it, and called it the pioneer modern architectural form. Its designer is, of course, anonymous.

Architect **John C. Parkin** in 1976

❦

Canadian literature is very interesting so long as you don't bother to read it.

Louis Dudek in 1976

❦

The only Canadian mythology is that there is a Canadian mythology.

Poet **Irving Layton** in 1977

❦

If I stayed in Canada I could have done very well. But nobody would have noticed.

David Clayton-Thomas of the rock group
Blood, Sweat and Tears

Canada does not win enough Nobel Prizes because the scientists and researchers don't know from one year to the next whether there will be sufficient funds for material, labs and assistants. If they worry, there can be no excellence, and therefore they cannot show results. Universities are not sardine factories or construction companies.

Linguist **Isaac Bar-Lewaw** in 1976

❀

The discovery of electro-magnetic waves had added a new facet to the struggle for self-assertion in Canada. Those waves are probably the strongest weapon in the arsenal of American imperialism. Other weapons can—at least theoretically—be combatted. Foreign films *could* be expropriated. Invading armies *could* be met along our unguarded frontier. Obsolescent manufactured junk *could* be blocked at border points. But radio waves are in the air everywhere. On the beaches, in the woods, in our bedrooms and basements—everywhere.

Playwright and media critic **Rick Salutin** in 1979

❀

Canadians, having become a wealthy nation without science, tend to think they can remain wealthy without science.

Nobel laureate physicist **John Polanyi** in 1979

❀

For most of us, writing in Canada, about Canada, for Canadian eyes, takes considerably more time and effort than, in any material sense, it is worth. Any cost-benefit study of the life of a writer in these parts would be brutally discouraging for those who imagine they might prosper from such a career.

Dalton Camp in 1981

You can't make a film just for the Canadian public; and, often, when you make a film just for the Canadian public, even the Canadian public doesn't want to see it.

Film director **Ivan Reitman** in 1980

❉

We yearn for our Mozarts, our Shakespeares and our Picassos. Nation-building is a matter of establishing links; and to the extent that the Great Artist is lacking, Canadians face the problem of a missing link.

Report of the Federal Cultural Policy
Review Committee, 1982

❉

Science today moves quickly. In the United States, the whole system, the whole national character encourages aggressive, ambitious, big science. That's why we have difficulty keeping scientists. We do good science in Canada, but not intrepid science.

Geneticist **Louis Siminovitch** in 1983

❉

The trap for journalists in this country is the same as for many others. Lacking real standards or independence, in envy they emulate Americans who may be better or worse, but are certainly richer and momentarily more famous. So their idea of leading Canadians is to follow Americans, their idea of originality is to be first to copy Americans, their knowledge of Canada is the United States divided by ten. What they desperately want is to be invited to the Big Apple in New York or Washington or Los Angeles, and the pity of it is for them, who needs more second-rate Americans?

Journalist **James Bacque** in the early 1980s

Financing a film in Canada is like trying to juggle a watermelon, a peach, and a pea at the same time. Just when you think you've got them all in the air, the pea slips through your fingers.

Film director **Ted Kotcheff**

＊

There are no stars in Canada. To have a star system you need the proper mechanics—an immense publicity industry, a public that wants stars, and a national point of view that encourages that idolizing. We have it in hockey, but practically nowhere else.

Actor **R. H. Thomson** in 1985

＊

Canadian culture is at the very front of the second rank.

Novelist **Barry Callaghan** in 1989

＊

It is nowhere written that a novelist must be upbeat or humanist. But it says something about Canadians that our most celebrated author [Margaret Atwood] creates novels which are mortuaries. They are full of acute recollection, but lifeless. Dialogue is wooden, spoken not by individuals but by strangulated puppets.

Globe and Mail arts critic **Ray Conlogue** in 1990

＊

The fey, angular gawkiness of Canadian movies has been so prevalent over the past two and a half decades that those of us who have overdosed on this material began to think that perhaps the Canadian personality really was that infantile and awkward.

Cultural critic **Bronwyn Drainie** in 1996

Every aspect of Canadian culture is endangered by the reality of sharing a continent with the U.S., a common language, and—most vital—an electronic network. All any advertiser in the U.S. has to do to invade every Canadian home is to switch on the power and start talking.

> Novelist **Sylvia Fraser** in a 1991 address
> at Harvard University

✦

If someone came up to me and asked me for advice, I'd tell them to stay away from the Canadian music business. It's full of politics and bureaucracy. It's trouble. Don't sign to a Canadian company. Don't sign to a Canadian publisher. Go south of the border, you'll get a better deal.

> Rock star **Bryan Adams** in 1992

✦

[It's] a unique example of success, proof that we don't have to be the backwater we're used to thinking we are.

> *Toronto Star* writer **Christopher Hume** in 1994,
> on the aura of sophistication from which
> Toronto would benefit with the Art Gallery of
> Ontario's decision to host a travelling exhibit,
> "From Cezanne to Matisse: Great French
> Paintings from The Barnes Foundation"

✦

We still don't have a national culture in the way our government intended; what we have are Canadians who share a common American culture.

> Writer **Susan Crean** in 1996

BUSINESS CONDITIONS

It is in vain to suppose that a free-trade system will be beneficial to a new and struggling colony which has nothing to export but raw materials. It is rather calculated to enrich an old commonwealth, whose people by their skill and labour make such raw materials valuable, and return them for consumption. The result of the system has been that the suppliers of the raw material at last become hewers of wood and drawers of water to the manufacturers.

Abraham Gesner, Halifax inventor of kerosene,
in 1849

❀

Canada's story begins in Lamentations and ends in Exodus.
Popular saying in Prince Edward Island in the
early 1880s among parents lamenting the
exodus of their children to better-paying jobs
elsewhere. "There is," noted the **Toronto _Mail_** in
1887, "scarcely a farmhouse in the older
provinces where there is not one empty chair
for the boy in the United States."

I have given you a faithful picture of a life in the backwoods of Canada, and I leave you to draw from it your own conclusions. To the poor, industrious working man it presents many advantages, to the poor gentleman, *none!*... If these sketches should prove the means of deterring one family from sinking their property, and shipwrecking all their hopes, by going to reside in the backwoods of Canada, I shall consider myself amply repaid for revealing the secrets of the prison-house, and feel that I have not toiled and suffered in vain.

Susanna Moodie, English emigrant and Ontario
pioneer settler, in her 1850s account,
Roughing It In The Bush

✦

We invent nothing.

Archibald MacMechan in a 1920 essay, "Canada
As Vassal State"

✦

More than any country in the world, Canada is the result of political, not economic, forces.

Journalist **John W. Dafoe** in 1935

✦

This is what came to me that night I bid Canada goodbye. If I died the succession duties would leave my family in the red, not the blue. True, I found the pot of gold at the end of the rainbow, and I found it in Canada. But I was paying out 80 per cent of the gold I'd found in taxes. Man don't work for that.

Mining magnate **Harry Oakes**, explaining his
1930s decision to exile himself to the
Bahamas in protest of Canada's
income-tax policies

Canadian nationalism was systematically encouraged and exploited by American capital. Canada moved from colony to nation to colony.

Political economist **Harold Innis** in 1948

✤

The deluge of U.S. investment funds—gushing across the border at the fantastic gross rate of almost three million dollars a day since 1945—has engulfed our profit-making enterprises to an extent that has reduced Canadians to holding squatters' rights in many industrial categories. American businessmen have appropriated more than three-quarters of our petroleum production, half of our manufacturing, mining and forest industries.

Peter C. Newman in his 1959 book, *Flame of Power: Intimate Profiles of Canada's Greatest Businessmen*

✤

Canadian nationalism! How old-fashioned can you get?

Tycoon and horse breeder **E. P. Taylor** in 1963

✤

The Canadian automobile industry settled down to being a pale copy of that of the United States. For some reason, Canada has never even developed cars suited to its climate. Sweden, a much smaller country, much less endowed with resources, has developed at least two outstanding automobiles—the Saab and the Volvo—both uniquely designed for the difficult Swedish climate, and both of these have enjoyed a good sale abroad, including Canada.

J. J. Brown in *Ideas in Exile: A History of Canadian Invention*, 1967

There are no spectacular choices in a country like Canada.
Pierre Trudeau in 1972, on limited options
for economic growth

✸

Canada is dependent on the United States for its culture, its economy, its defence and its baby alligators. In contrast, the only thing that the States really needs from Canada is water. Some U.S. senators believe that if a way can be found to rid Canada of its impurities (the Canadian people), the country has tremendous potential as a reservoir.

Eric Nicol

✸

Canada is like a farmer who maintains his high standard of living by selling off another piece of the farm every spring.
Former federal finance minister **Walter Gordon**
in 1975, bemoaning Canada's reliance on
raw-material exports

✸

If you want to be on the ninety-fifth floor, with global horizons, you must go to New York; the highest one can go in Canada is the fifty-fourth floor.
Future federal industry minister **Herb Gray** in
1972, at a time when the Toronto-Dominion
Tower, with fifty-four floors, was
Canada's tallest building

✸

There are some parts of Canada still owned by Canadians, but they are too scattered to make a country.
Louis Dudek in 1975

Some sixty years ago Sir Wilfrid Laurier declared that the twentieth century belongs to Canada. By the middle of the century it had become clear that Canada belongs to the United States.

Economic nationalist **Kari Levitt** in *Silent Surrender: The Multinational Corporation in Canada*, 1970

✦

Poor old Canada, at once so big and yet so small, the Gulliver of the North with no visible means of enforcing its will.

Peter C. Newman, on Canada's weakness in asserting its position in trade disputes

✦

If Edison had lived in Nova Scotia, you might be reading this by candlelight.

Tom Gray, former director of the Atlantic Industrial Research Institute, in 1976, criticizing the lack of scientific entrepreneurship in Canada

✦

Like Brutus, John Diefenbaker was a honourable man. He just suffered from the widespread national disease of lack of self-confidence, of suspicion of everything that rises above mediocrity. The cancellation of the Arrow was a symptom of that national ill.

York University military affairs expert **John Gellner** in 1980, on federal government's 1959 decision to scrap development of the Avro Arrow jet fighter plane, Canada's most high-profile industrial and engineering project of its time

Among the developed countries, Canada is absolutely unique in the way it is operated as a subsidiary business.

> **Robert Blair**, CEO of the Alberta pipeline firm Nova Corp., in 1977, despairing of Canada's branch-plant economy, in which most major business decisions are made by foreigners

✤

It's not Canadian to be competitive and imaginative. You have to watch out. You might reward the tough competitor, the guy who comes up with the different, imaginative way of doing things.

> Toronto broadcaster **Dick Smythe** in the early 1980s, reacting to a federal regulator's decision to ban a planned promotional offer of a free limousine ride for airline customers

✤

If Canada invented the wheel, it would drag it on a sled to be marketed in the United States.

> Technology industries commentator **Denzil Doyle** in 1985

✤

They [the federal government] are creating debt—a great amount of debt—for future generations and putting a burden on our children that they will not be able to cope with.

> **Robert Campeau** in 1988, chastising governments for failing to control their spending and for creating regulatory burdens more irksome in Canada than in the U.S. Two years later, the bankruptcy of Campeau's overleveraged Federated Department Stores brought down his retailing and real estate empire

It was widely felt, probably accurately, that average Canadians were less interested in enterprise and risk-taking than Americans, less distrustful of authority and organizations, more interested in security and a quiet life. Perhaps the business bestsellers told the comparative story: *In Search of Excellence* in the United States, *The Best 100 Companies to Work for in Canada.*

Business historian Michael Bliss in 1987

❀

In the United States, they run with the ball. In Canada, we apply for a government grant to get the money to buy the ball.

Geraldine Kenney-Wallace, chemist, physicist
and future chair of the Science Council
of Canada, in 1986, on the slow pace at
which Canadian business exploits
technological innovations

❀

Probably because of our ancient, self-imposed status as a branch-plant country well back in the baggage train of the Anglo-Americans, we have come to regard achievements, other than by professional athletes and geriatrics, as somehow un-Canadian.

Conrad Black in 1986

❀

Canada is a gigantic loophole through which billions of dollars' worth of drugs and dirty money pass annually. Canada is a smuggler's and money launderer's paradise.

Journalist Diane Francis in
Contrapreneurs, 1988

This country is too damn wealthy for its own good, and has not been forced to make the tough decisions. We cannot give everybody everything they want. We've not said that ever before, but we should say it if we want to be viable. Canada's like me. Wealthy. But I hope I have more discipline than the country has.

Liquor magnate and sometime Montreal
Expos part owner **Charles Bronfman** of Seagram
Co. Ltd. in 1990, on a Canadian economy
dragged down by government indebtedness

✦

Our quest for an industry independent of the Americans has given us a prime rate five points above that of the U.S.; top tax rates almost twenty points higher; a sharply higher price index; a growing and proportionately much larger public-sector deficit, despite the American defence burden; and only 70 per cent of the U.S. standard of living, despite the unique problems of the American black underclass.

Conrad Black in 1990

✦

The entire country, apart from Ontario, has a special government agency or department within Industry Canada to look after its interests and pursue special treatment ... We cannot object to strategies that help other parts of Canada become economically stronger. But there is something troubling about the fact that, as the federal government divides up shrinking science and technology and industrial development dollars, there is no one at the table to watch for Ontario's interest.

Toronto Star economics columnist **David Crane**
in 1996, questioning the fairness of regional
economic development programs

Life has been hard here. Let no one sentimentalize it—
Newfoundland is a very physical place. Its population is stag-
nant or in decline. The climate is awful, the land is rocky,
resources are scarce. Our best industry is fishing and it's *never*
been good. We've had very few periods of prosperity; our
economy has always been down or trembling on the edge.

Newfoundland author Patrick O'Flaherty in 1991

✤

We're in the early stages of bankruptcy. Interest rates are going
north, the dollar is going south. The people are scared that
the marvellous Canadian experiment is failing before their
very eyes.

James Gray, president of Calgary's Canadian
Hunter Exploration, in 1992

✤

The feds are a fairly neutral—I was going to say neutered—
player.

Warren Jestin, chief economist at the Bank of
Nova Scotia, in 1992, on the inability of the
federal government to prop up the economy

✤

If you have some money in Canada, why would you dig a
foundation, put up a building, buy machines and cope with
the bureaucratic environment, when you can buy government bonds? No risk, no bureaucracy.

Auto-parts czar Frank Stronach of Magna
International Inc. in 1995

✤

Sigh ... Another day—another 84.7 cents.

Cartoonist Edd Uluschak on the devalued loonie

THE BODY IMPOLITIC

I would be quite willing, personally, to leave that whole [Hudson's Bay Co.] country a wilderness for the next half century, but I fear if Englishmen do not go there, Yankees will.

John A. Macdonald in 1865, on Western Canada

❀

The political destiny of our country seems to be involved in utter uncertainty and impenetrable obscurity.

Education reformer **Egerton Ryerson** in 1865

❀

At present we have for a population of four millions, eight kings, one central and seven provincial, as many parliaments, and sixty-five ministers of the crown; while England is content with a single king, a single parliament—the members of which are not paid—and a single cabinet, seldom containing as many members as the cabinet at Ottawa. We have also judges and chief-justices as the stars of heaven in number.

Goldwin Smith in 1880

To make a nation there must be a common life, common sentiments, common aims, and common hopes. Of these, in the case of Quebec and Ontario, there are none.

Goldwin Smith in 1889

❦

This is a difficult country to govern.

Wilfrid Laurier in 1905

❦

There is Ontario patriotism, Quebec patriotism, or Western patriotism, each based on the hope that it may swallow up the others, but there is no Canadian patriotism, and we can have no Canadian nation when we have no Canadian patriotism.

Henri Bourassa, *Le Devoir* publisher and Quebec nationalist, in 1907

❦

Canada stands practically alone in modern, self-governing democratic countries in her inability to change her constitution in accordance with what may be the development of political thought.

Former federal cabinet minister **Clifford Sifton** in 1922

❦

An honest attempt to enumerate the points in which our Canadian civilization differs from that of the United States is apt to be almost as brief as the famous essay upon snakes in Ireland.

Frank Underhill in 1929

We are plagued with false political phrases. We are supposed
to be associated with the British Commonwealth of Nations,
although no such thing exists. We are alleged to be part of a
third British Empire, although there never was more than one,
and we have ceased to be part of it. We are called a dominion,
although we have become a kingdom. We are said to be a confederation, although we are a federation. We have ten governments, but not one of them has any governing authority.

John S. Ewart, Ottawa lawyer and
constitutional expert, in 1933

✿

Democracy, as measured by the franchise, came to Canada
almost by stealth; certainly not as an army with banners.

W. L. Morton in 1943

✿

Like most Canadians I'm indifferent to the visit of the Queen
… We're a little annoyed at still being dependent.

Joyce Davidson, TV talk-show host, in a
1959 interview on the U.S. television
program, the *Today Show*

✿

We French, we English, never lost our
    civil war,
endure it still, a bloodless civil bore

Earle Birney in 1962

✿

Quebec is not a province like the others. It is a little more
stupid.

Le Devoir editor **Gerard Filion**, on Quebec's
role in Confederation

Federation in 1867 became the instrument for westward expansion. It was the political expedient for bringing the West under the control of the St. Lawrence Valley.

R.G. Riddell, on alienation in Western
Canada, in 1940

❦

Historically, French Canadians have not really believed in democracy for themselves; and English Canadians have not really wanted it for others. Such are the foundations upon which our two ethnic groups have absurdly pretended to be building democratic forms of government.

Pierre Trudeau in 1964

❦

As Canadians we attempted a ridiculous task in trying to build a conservative nation in the age of progress, on a continent we share with the most dynamic nation on earth.

Philosopher **George P. Grant** in 1965

❦

I've always felt the reason we are so unemotional about our beginning is that Confederation was a constitutional development, and not the result of a popular revolution. If we had only hated George III it might have been different.

Frank MacKinnon, former president of the
University of Prince Edward Island

❦

Confederation is genocide without end.

André d'Allemagne in *Le colonialisme
au Quebec*, 1966

Canada is a country whose major problems are never solved.
A.R.M. Lower in 1967

❈

We had spent a hundred years trying to become a nation; now we were a nation and it was hell.
Peter C. Newman in 1968

❈

Quebec is one of the ten provinces against which Canada is defending itself.
Carl Dubuc in 1968

❈

What confronts us is either the breaking-up of our country or its continuance as a fragmented, decentralized nation, firmly integrated in the American economic and military empire, with all its assets, down to the last treasures of its birthright, freely expendable in the service of the government and people of the United States.
Historian **Donald Creighton** in 1970

❈

The Canadian kid who wants to grow up to be prime minister isn't thinking big, he is setting a limit on his ambitions rather early.
Mordecai Richler in 1971

❈

Canada is a collection of ten provinces with strong governments loosely connected by fear.
Dave Broadfoot

How did Canada come apart? The question has puzzled historians, though not as much as how to get the silver wrapper off Swiss cheese.

Eric Nicol in the 1977 book, *Canada Cancelled Because of Lack of Interest*

❦

The Canadian confederation was nothing more than a vast financial transaction carried out by the bourgeoisie at the expense of the workers of the country, and more especially the workers of Quebec.

Pierre Vallières in 1971

❦

It's not Pierre Trudeau and the Liberal party who haven't been able to knit this country together ... It's the whole of Canada, it's the industries, the head offices of corporations, it's the people who complain they can't find housing or jobs in Metro Toronto. They can find them in Saskatchewan, if they want to move there.

Pierre Trudeau in 1974 on regional alienation

❦

The real works of art in Canada are the annual reports of corporations and Federal Royal Commissions where the distortion of fact to verify a central mythology would make Shakespeare's history plays look like the work of an amateur.

Author **Dave Godfrey** in 1977

❦

Two things hold this country together. Everybody hates Air Canada coffee, and everybody hates Ontario.

Newfoundland premier **Brian Peckford** in 1979

Well, it still is a good place to live. But that's all Canada is—just a good place to live. Canadians have lost their destiny, you know.

Donald Creighton in 1979

◆

By unspoken agreement, Canadian citizenship carries the ultimate freedom: the freedom to declare that one doesn't want to be Canadian, to urge that one's region should forthwith cease to be part of Canada, and yet to go on being a Canadian and receiving the appropriate benefits. No Quebec or Alberta separatist, so far as I know, has been denied a federal welfare payment or even a Canada Council grant because of his or her desire to separate.

Robert Fulford in 1982

◆

In terms of our proportionate NATO expenditures, we now rank at the bottom—except for Iceland, which has no armed forces at all.

Peter C. Newman in 1983

◆

Given any form of incursion by foreign troops into the Canadian Arctic—providing we ever found out about it—we could do nothing except send a mountie out in a Ski Doo to give out parking tickets.

Peter C. Newman in 1983

◆

This is a difficult country to govern.

Prime Minister **Brian Mulroney** in 1986

While Canada is not in any way the "difficult country to govern" it is often claimed to be, since it is inherently orderly,
democratic, and affluent, it is an almost impossible country
to lead.

Journalist **Richard Gwyn** in 1985

❦

For me, Canada is made up of two losers, face-to-face, feeling we count for nothing. It's a huge shelf on which two peoples were put and forgotten a long time ago. And there they
are, preserved in ice. The question is, what are we going to
do about it?

Quebec dramatist **René-Daniel Dubois** in 1986

❦

Eventually, anglophones will question the value of the Quebec
connection. The Quebec issue in Canadian politics may
become not whether Quebec will secede—but whether it
should be expelled.

Journalist **Peter Brimelow** in 1986

❦

Canada is a nation of sum-keepers, each province and region
ready aye ready with its tally of debts and profits over time.
Not every country has its price, but Canadians are quick to
assert this one does, often with a grimace and snarl. Historians
talk of an 1867 "Confederation bargain"—with railroads an
early condition of union—and the coin-counting has never
ceased.

William Thorsell in 1986

The thing that keeps this great country together is that everybody hates Ontario; and the thing that keeps Ontario together is that everybody hates Toronto; and the thing that keeps Toronto together is that everyone hates Bay Street.

Ontario premier **David Peterson**

✦

When Albertans flaunted bumper stickers saying, "Let the eastern bastards freeze in the dark," it didn't comfort Maritimers that the target was Ontario, because that meant Westerners didn't even know where the real east was. The real east was Down Home, and its people would rather be bastards than nobodies.

Journalist **Harry Bruce** in 1988

✦

We are the orphans of Confederation and we resent it. Watch the irrelevance and insignificance and colonialism with which Western Canada is portrayed on national television.

Broadcasting mogul **Israel H. (Izzy) Asper** in
1989, vowing that his CanWest Global chain
of TV stations would be pledged to ensuring
that Western Canada isn't depicted as simply
"some farmer with a straw hat in his mouth
standing by a tractor saying: 'Gosh the
grasshoppers are bad this year.'"

✦

Independence requires the power, on our own, to hurt an aggressor. Until we acquire our own nuclear deterrrent, we will be wards of our enemies.

Essayist **David Frum** in 1990

As the monopoly supplier of health-care resources, the government is also the effective monopoly employer of health-care personnel. Accordingly, it periodically must negotiate collective agreements with the almost entirely unionized health-care sector, including fee schedules with physicians and other providers of covered services. Sometimes these negotiations go smoothly and there are no interruptions of health-care services. With increasing frequency, however, the negotiations do not go smoothly—in part because the governments involved are finding it very difficult to keep the lid on health-care costs without putting them in direct conflict with health-care providers and support staffs ... It is questionable under the circumstances whether the U.S. should look to Canada for solutions to health-care problems.

> **Michael Walker**, executive director
> of Vancouver's Fraser Institute, a
> conservative think tank, writing in *The
> Wall Street Journal* in 1991

❖

There's nothing easier in Canada than to unite most of Canada against part of Canada.

> Former prime minister **Joe Clark** in 1991

❖

There's so much misinformation. People are convinced that Quebec gets everything and are astonished when I tell them that Saskatchewan gets, per capita, ten times as much. I have a sense of despair about it.

> Saskatoon MP **Chris Axworthy** in 1991, on perceptions that federal spending is unequally shared among regions

We know who our friends and enemies are—after Quebec and
Ontario, the rest [of the provinces] are not very important.
                    Marcil Dutil, Montreal business executive and
                              Quebec nationalist, in 1991

※

Canadians massively rejected each other.
                         Gretta Chambers, chancellor of McGill
                              University, on the rejection of the
                           Charlottetown constitutional accord in
                                  a 1992 national referendum

※

We are in some ways the cheap date of NATO.
                    Former defence minister **Kim Campbell**, in 1993,
                          arguing against cuts in Canada's spending on
                                military commitments in Europe

※

We are one of the white races that has the least children.
                    Future Quebec premier **Lucien Bouchard** in 1995,
                                on Quebec's low birthrate

※

We are condemned to live together.
                         Alain Dexter, radio talk-show host in Alma,
                         Que., reflecting sourly on the results of the
                         1995 Quebec referendum on sovereignty

Since referendum day, I have seen literally one hundred media reports flailing the victors—the pro-Canada side. In that same time, I have not seen one report on how the secessionists were beaten. Instead our media have essentially declared the losing separatists triumphant. Something is wrong here. No wonder the nation is so gloomy. When you win and you're still declared a loser—this can only happen in Canada—it makes for a tough Christmas season.

Jean Chrétien biographer **Lawrence Martin**
in 1995

♣

In most epic battles—Waterloo, the Spanish Armada, Gettysburg—there is a clear winner and a loser. When Wolfe climbed the cliffs to the Plains of Abraham and beat Montcalm, the French thought it was a tie. The distinguished American historian Henry Steele Commager has written that never in the history of colonial wars "has the victor treated the vanquished so generously." It has resulted in "the Canadian way." Why did the Canadian cross the road? To get to the middle …

Allan Fotheringham in 1995, response to the
outcome of the Quebec referendum

♣

The Parti Quebecois and Bloc Quebecois are yet others in a long line of whining regional special interest groups that have risen to plague the broad Canadian political system that includes Western farmers, Eastern fishermen and others. [PQ leader Jacques] Parizeau and [BQ leader Lucien] Bouchard are just skilled at griping a little louder than most.

Greg Burch of Winnipeg in a 1995 *Time*
letter to the editor

I was caught off guard at the big unity rally in Montreal. I had expected the worst—staged expressions of patriotism are almost always maudlin. But the No side drew a crowd straight out of Christmas, all geniality and goodwill. The only time I felt at all uncomfortable was when the big flag came my way. You probably saw, on television or in news photos, an enormous Canadian flag afloat on a sea of people. Actually the flag was moving hand-to-hand over the crowd at quite a clip. As it came directly overhead of me a hearty chant went up. I could tell the chant had three beats, and that the beats rhymed, but I couldn't make sense of them. I figured it must be a francophone thing.

"What are they chanting?" I asked a colleague.

"Canada," he said.

Saturday Night editor **Kenneth Whyte**, relating his brush with Canadian patriotism a few days before the 1995 Quebec sovereignty vote

✦

I'm uneasy with the Western separatist label, but I really feel that this action has broken my faith in the national government.

Roger Gibbins, University of Calgary political scientist, in 1995, appalled by a federal initiative to grant B.C., but not Alberta, a constitutional veto

✦

If Quebec does indeed opt for separation, I believe I speak for many Canadians by inquiring if there is any possibility they would take Toronto with them and leave us Montreal.

Eric M. Wright of Fredericton, in a 1995 letter to *The Globe and Mail*

Every time this province makes a move, we get kicked in the ... well, you know. The federal politicos remain hypnotized by the idea Ottawa can force everybody to sing caringly and sharingly from their Just Society song-sheet. Meanwhile, Ottawa fiddles while the country burns.

> Calgary Sun columnist **Rick Bell** in 1995, dismayed at Ottawa's efforts to block extra-billing for medical services in Alberta, and saying if Alberta were to have its own sovereignty referendum, he'd vote Yes: "We only fork over more to this thing called Confederation than any other province. Give us our power."

❀

Only English-Canadians are here alone, emotionally and psychically. [All the rest] are linked to their ancestral homeland.

> **Richard Gwyn** in his 1995 book *Nationalism Without Walls: The Unbearable Lightness of Being Canadian*, in which he cites multiculturalism as a factor in Canada's lack of unity

❀

When you have a huge country with vast distances between major pockets of population it means that the majority does not just rule, it oppresses. Central Canada utterly controls the government of Canada. B.C.'s chronic disaffection underscores the basic ills of a nineteenth-century foreign system imposed in federal form on a huge country with a widely spread population.

Rafe Mair in 1996

Living with the Quebec issue is not like "a trip to the dentist" in Jacques Parizeau's colourful phrase. A trip to the dentist ends. Living with the Quebec issue is more like a battle against cancer: It goes on and on with no certainty about the outcome.

William Thorsell in 1996

❦

Canada, the country that dares not speak its name.

Philip Resnick, political science professor at the University of British Columbia, in 1996, on Ottawa's chronic timidity in allowing Quebec nationalists to dictate federal policies

❦

We're still a long way from not looking after people, but it has to be watched because of ... the decline of collectivity in this country. We seem to be becoming increasingly Americanized, which imposes a rugged and un-Canadian individualism on our ethic.

Former Alberta premier **Peter Lougheed** in 1995, on the threat to Canada's social-safety net posed by deficit cutting

IDENTITY CRISIS

You rule yourselves as fully as any people in the world, while in your foreign affairs, your relations with other countries, whether peaceful or warlike, commercial or financial, or otherwise, you may have no more voice than the people of Japan.

> Canada West statesman **Edward Blake** in an 1874 Ontario speech

♦

Canadian nationality being a lost cause, the ultimate union of Canada and the United States appears now to be morally certain; so that nothing is left for Canadian patriotism but to provide that it shall be a union indeed, and not an annexation.

> **Goldwin Smith** in 1878

♦

We French-Canadians belong to one country, Canada; Canada is for us the whole world; but the English-Canadians have two countries, one here and one across the sea.

> **Wilfrid Laurier**

We have never had enough national spirit to provide ourselves with a distinctive flag; we have people in Canada
objecting to standing up when "O Canada" is sung, we have
trifled with the question of citizenship and nationality until
the young Canadian is never quite sure whether he is a
Canadian or a Hottentot because he had a Hottentot grand-
mother. We have put enthusiasm into every national day but
our own ... For all this we have ourselves to blame.

John W. Dafoe in 1921

❦

Canada's first nationalist was shot and ever since the
Dominion's political leaders have diluted their Canadianism
with imperialism. There has been no fear of another assassi-
nation: there has been dread of political suicide.

Future *Saturday Night* editor **Robert
Farquharson** in 1931 noting the impact of
D'Arcy McGee's death, likely at the hands
of a Fenian extremist, in 1868

❦

It does not matter what the surface civilization may be in
Canada; it is from this great country overseas that you got the
source of your civilization. There in the little winding lanes
which lead around to the Red Lion and the Crown and
Anchor; there in the little villages scattered all over, and
there along the muddy banks of the Thames lie the germs of
our civilization here.

Beverley Baxter, Toronto-born journalist
and British MP, in a 1932 Empire Club
of Canada speech

We have a habit of continually worrying about problems of other countries in order to keep from worry about our own.

Harold Innis in 1939

❦

In Canada we have enough to do keeping up with the two spoken languages without trying to invent slang, so we just go right ahead and use English for literature, Scotch for sermons and American for conversation.

Stephen Leacock in 1942

❦

America's attic, an empty room,
a something possible, a chance, a dance
that is not danced. A cold kingdom.

Patrick Anderson, "Poem on Canada," 1946

❦

Why is it we have no Canadian jokes—I mean the kind I could tell over the radio? Why is there no joke about the Canadian, much as you hear about the Irishman, the Scotsman, the American?

Broadcaster **John Fisher** in 1947

❦

To say Canada is young is to say we're eighteen million Peter Pans incapable of growing up. The trouble is we're too old. We grew up saying no—no to the United States and French revolutions, no to Papineau when he wanted to introduce U.S. democracy. We're afraid now if we say yes to U.S. ideas we'll wake up some morning and find there isn't any difference between us and the U.S.

Frank Underhill in 1961

As if he had not heard, the admiral stormed on, "You sold your birthright, then went searching for it with talk about distinctive Canadianism. Well, there was a Canadianism once, but you got soft and lost it, and not all your Royal Commissions piled on end will ever find it now."

Arthur Hailey in his 1962 novel *In High Places*, in which a U.S. admiral lectures a Canadian prime minister

*

If we are eventually to satisfy ourselves that we have at last achieved a Canadian identity, it will be only when we are satisfied that we have arrived at a better American way of life than the Americans have.

Frank Underhill in 1964

*

O Canada! We don't know what you are.
Nation, we thought, but that Quebec doth bar.
And a colony you had ceased to be,
So we know what you are not;
And we stand on guard,
Though it's rather hard,
When we're not quite sure for what.
O Canada! Great Undefined!
O Canada! Can't you make up your mind?
O Canada! Can't you some status find?

Constitutional expert **Eugene Forsey** in 1967, inspired by Ottawa's objection to the use of the word "national" in the name of one of the Centennial organizations

We in Toronto are curiously apathetic towards our history in terms of landmarks, street names and the like; indeed, surely no city in the world with a background of three hundred years does so little to make that background known. Our children are brought up to take pride in the British beginnings of the city, but they have a limited knowledge of that vastly more exciting period when the Senecas had a village on the site, when black-robed priests and French noblemen went at times to the mouth of the Humber and wrote glowing letters home to France of the potentialities of Toronto as a settlement in the empire of Louis XIV. No pageants recall the great events that took place under the French regime; 1959 passed with little comment on the destruction of Fort Rouille in 1759, and yet, in the opinion of historians, this was the birthplace of a metropolis that now boasts a million and a half souls. M. Pierre Roy, the Quebec archivist, was moved to say of Fort Rouille, "this is the great city of Toronto in embryo— Paris did not have a more glorious beginning."

Author and architectural preservationist
Eric Arthur in *No Mean City*, 1964

❦

I have strong feelings about Canada, by the way. Not, however, so strong that I intend to let them become a source of endless humiliation. I am not among those who believe that Canada was created by God. It became a nation because of the vainglory of the English; because of the treachery of the French (who could have protected their colonists easily); because of the incompetence of the Americans (who were on the verge of capturing the country twice); and because of the enslavement and virtual extinction of the Hurons, Iroquois and Algonquins.

Maclean's editor **Ralph Allen** in 1965

The only difference between Quebec and Rhodesia is the colour of our skin.

> Quebec nationalist **René Lévesque** in 1967,
> comparing the condition of Quebec
> francophones with the repression endured
> by the majority black population of
> modern-day Zimbabwe

❋

We moved from British influence to American influence without much feeling of purely national identity in between.

> **Lester Pearson** in 1967

❋

My generation of Canadians grew up believing that if we were very good or very smart, or both, we would someday graduate from Canada.

> **Robert Fulford**

❋

Having overheard that Leonard Cohen's TV film was titled *I Am A Hotel*, his oldest friend murmured: "Praise the Lord. Here at last is one Canadian who doesn't have an identity problem."

> Poet **Irving Layton**

❋

Imagine a Canadian Dream, which implied that everybody in the world ought to share it! Imagine a Committee of UnCanadian Activities! You can't. UnCanadianism is almost the very definition of Canadianism.

> Novelist **Hugh Hood** in 1968

The American says, "My country, right or wrong." The Canadian: "My country, but what are the other options?"

Eric Nicol

♦

Without at least a touch of anti-Americanism, Canada would have no reason to exist. Of all general definitions of the Canadians, this is the most nearly valid: twenty million people who, for anything up to twenty million reasons, prefer not to be Americans.

Journalist **Blair Fraser** in 1967

♦

The Canadian identity is bound up with the feeling that the end of the rainbow never falls on Canada.

Northrop Frye

♦

A statue symbolizing Canadian patriotism would portray someone holding his breath and crossing his fingers.

Northrop Frye

♦

One is tempted to conclude, in fact, that there could not be a Canada without the United States—and may not be a Canada with one.

J. M. S. Careless

♦

Only the favoured few—the nationalist intellectuals themselves—are free from that colonialist mentality which permanently blinds Canadians to their real status as a colonized people.

Historian **Ramsey Cook** in 1970

Canada is a land of no one ideology, no single vision; it is a cultural freeport, a way station for travellers (who often move on soon to the other America), a no-man's-land even, or at least no abiding city, a place not easily confused with paradise or the promised land. This "indigestible Canada," this Marx Brothers' Fredonia, this Austro-Hungary of the new world, with its two official peoples and its multitude of permitted ones, its ethnic islands and cultural archipelagos, its ghettos of the unpasteurized and unhomogenized, this harbour of old Adams unable or unwilling to be reborn or to burn just yet their old European clothes.

Historian **William Kilbourn** in 1970

✿

And this is a country where the young
   leave quickly
unwilling to know what their fathers
   know

Al Purdy, from *Selected Poems*, 1972

✿

Canada, with its empty spaces, its largely unknown lakes and rivers and islands, its division of language, its dependence on immense railways to hold it physically together, has had this peculiar problem of an obliterated environment throughout most of its history. The effects of this are clear in the curiously abortive cultural developments of Canada ... They are shown even more clearly in its present lack of will to resist its own disintegration, in the fact that it is practically the only country left in the world which is a pure colony, colonial in psychology as well as in mercantile economics.

Northrop Frye in 1971

If you've gone through public school and had boring Canadian history shoved at you, you'd realize that nothing really interesting has ever gone on in Canada. When I found out that John A. Macdonald was a juicer I thought that was terrific. So what else is there? Nelson Eddy, Jeanette MacDonald and Laura Secord running through the woods.

Actor **Michael Sarrazin** in 1970

❖

I just got signed to star in the Canadian version of the movie *Fame*. It's titled *Total Obscurity*.

Briane Naismok

❖

In order to be psychologically well, and in order to be fully creative, I think people need a strong political identity, a sense of territory. I don't even think it's a question that can be debated, it's a biographical imperative. Quebec would not appear so disruptive to the, shall I say, order of Canada, if the rest of Canada were equally strong and concerned with its future.

Actress **Genevieve Bujold** in 1973

❖

It is still Canada's problem to convince foreigners—and to some extent its own people—that it is for real.

John W. Holmes in 1974

❖

Surely Canada is the only country in the world in which students travel thousands of miles just so they can sit outdoors in strange cities to try to sort out why their nation is not what they want it to be.

Harry Bruce in 1977

Canadians of my generation, sprung to adolescence during World War Two, were conditioned to believe that the world happened elsewhere. And now, suddenly, we are a *bona fide* trouble spot.

> **Mordecai Richler** in 1977, reacting to the
> Parti Quebecois victory in the 1976
> Quebec election

❖

Happy nations, someone said, have no history—an aphorism of possible consolation to Canadians.

> **Dalton Camp** in 1980

❖

Canada is, then, a loose federation of nation states, held tenuously together more by VIA Rail and the CBC than by a universally shared history and destiny.

> Journalist **Wayne Grady** in 1981

❖

The curious fact is that, in order to qualify as Canadians, we are not required to be loyal, even in theory, to the idea of Canada.

> **Robert Fulford** in 1982

❖

In the U.S., they suffer through a House Un-American Activities Committee because they not only know who they're supposed to be, but insist on it. Such a committee in Canada would be laughable. We still refuse to agree on what are the words to our national anthem.

> **Barry Callaghan**

People's eyes glaze over when you say, "Canada." Maybe we should invade South Dakota or something.

> **Sondra Gotlieb**, wife of the former Canadian
> ambassador to the U.S., in 1982

❧

But it's even more true that unless we speak out when we do have something to say, we will indeed become an international neuter. "Finlandized" is beginning to slip out of the language. Unless [Prime Minister Brian] Mulroney develops a coherent and distinctively Canadian foreign policy, no matter the annoyance this may cause in Washington, that word may start to be replaced by a new term of diplomatic derision—to be "Canadianized."

> **Richard Gwyn** in 1984

❧

"I'm not an American. I'm a Canadian."
"There's a difference," Hanna said, "but I keep forgetting what it is."

> Author **Matt Cohen** in "Golden Whore of the
> Heartland," 1986

❧

Some tinpot dictator can command infinitely more attention in the United States and in Congress than can a tremendous ally and friend like Canada.

> Prime Minister **Brian Mulroney** in a 1986
> U.S. television interview

Canada's inferiority complex stems from a colonial mentality. Successful colonization consists of convincing the natives that whatever they have or can produce is *a priori* inferior to the culture, skill, and standards of the colonial power. The British were masters at this. They managed with brutal charm and incredible arrogance to walk into many colonies of older culture and convince them they weren't worth anything. The Scots were dumped on as the poor white trash at home, so they came over here to dump on someone else and pass on this terrible repression. The Americans were smart and got out of that. But I can never understand here how a country, even before it starts, accepts that it is not as good as the guy next door. When I was little back in Hungary, we were taught that the world is God's hat and Hungary is the bouquet on it. That's a pile of BS, of course. It's flowers mixed with weeds, but you're taught to believe you are special. You are here on earth to do something and take pleasure and pride in doing it the best you can. You don't start off being spiritually and psychically retarded, believing you are less than everyone else. If I had enough money I'd send Canada to a good shrink for twenty years.

> **John Hirsch**, artistic director of the Stratford
> Shakespearean Festival, quoted in Andrew H.
> Malcolm's *The Canadians*

❦

Born on the First of July. A Canadian War Picture. The gripping story of a Canadian soldier faithfully serving his country in peace-torn Cyprus. Then, one unforgettable and tragic night, an event happens that forever changes his life. He cuts his lip in a bizarre drinking accident. He must spend the rest of his life trying to cope with his handicap.

> **Royal Canadian Air Farce** sketch

When will the time come to prove that we are a substantial power in the world, and not an adolescent impersonation of the pure snow-maiden of the north imagining she is being lusted after by a ravening American dragon?

Conrad Black in 1987

✦

Canada is not so much a country as a holding tank filled with the disgruntled progeny of defeated peoples. French Canadians consumed by self-pity; the descendants of Scots who fled the Duke of Cumberland; Irish the famine; the Jews the Black Hundreds ... Most of us are still huddled tight to the border, looking into the candy store window, scared by the Americans on one side and the bush on the other.

Mordecai Richler in 1989

✦

Canadians are so incredibly insecure that somewhere in his psyche every single Canadian has a feeling that people in the United States have some kind of visceral, cultural and life experiences he does not have. If you're Canadian, you think about a person from the States as the brother who went to sea, caught the clap and made a million dollars in Costa Rica or Hong Kong.

Donald Sutherland

✦

In my view, there isn't any one Canadian identity. Canada has no national culture.

Sheila Finestone, federal minister of multiculturalism, in 1995, in a controversial response to critics of government policies that promote multiculturalism

What do Quebeckers know about English Canada's culture? Not very much ... Because of the common language, Canadian art is often mistaken for American art. Is there any way to tell that pop singers like Robbie Robertson, Bryan Adams or Blue Rodeo are not American? If k.d. lang is known as an Albertan, isn't this mainly because of her controversial ads against eating beef?

Quebec political columnist **Lysiane Gagnon**
in 1991

✦

Canadians don't feel part of this country unless they're out of it. There's nothing to link a person from Winnipeg with someone from Quebec, unless they're in Venice together, sitting in St. Mark's Square drinking cappuccino. Suddenly you have something in common.

Theatre director **Robert Lepage** in 1990

✦

If what we have in common is our diversity, do we really have anything in common at all? ... What has held our country together is not commitment to shared ideology, but rather a tenuous willingness to co-exist.

University of Lethbridge sociologist
Reginald W. Bibby in 1990

✦

Why we even exist as a country, and whether we ought to do so, is our national preoccupation. Stereotyping and a general lack of exposure to each other make it easier to forge barriers than bonds. This angst is not exclusively Canadian, but we do seem to have elevated it to the pathological.

Montreal writer **Ted Hoffman** in 1995

Surely, some nations do not deserve to exist. What is it about the Canadian species that qualifies it for preservation? The idea of Canada—the animating principle which alone allows us to believe that this existence is the right one—has long since disappeared. Whatever was noble or true or even coherent about Canada as an idea was beaten out of it years ago.

Columnist **Andrew Coyne** in 1994

♦

For some reason, Lucien Bouchard seems to have set a few people's teeth on edge with his comment that "Canada is divisible because Canada is not a real country."

Canada has always been divisible. We define ourselves by our divisibleness: We can grow to our full potential only if we get the constitutional agreement of seven of ten provinces representing 50 per cent of the population and subdivided by two provinces from each of five regions, some of which have one, three or four components, *and* a majority in the Senate, *and* when the moon is in the seventh house and Jupiter is aligned with Mars.

Bouchard is probably right on the money when he says Canada is not a real country. It is but a gift of the imagination.

Columnist **Robert Sheppard** in 1996

♦

It's not a country you love. It's a country you worry about.

Robertson Davies on Canada

PART **TWO**

The Natural
Superiority
of Canada

*How Others
See Us*

THE LAND

Nature was so generous here that it seemed to them no cattle would need any winter fodder, but could graze outdoors. There was no frost in winter, and the grass hardly withered. The days and nights were more nearly equal than in Greenland or Iceland. On the shortest day of winter the sun was up between breakfast time and late afternoon.

Leif Ericsson, Viking explorer in approximately 1001, describing the site of L'Anse aux Meadows, Nfld., which has been designated as a World Heritage Site by the United Nations

✤

As fine land as it is possible to see.

Explorer **Jacques Cartier** in 1534, claiming all of Canada for France

✤

It [is] fine land with large fields covered with corn … in the middle of these fields stands the village of Hochelaga.

French explorer **Jacques Cartier** in 1535, describing the present-day site of Montreal

Love, which I have always cherished for the exploration of New France, has made me desirous of extending more and more my travels over the country, in order, by means of its numerous rivers, lakes, and streams, to obtain at last a complete knowledge of it.

French explorer **Samuel de Champlain** in 1603

✦

[There are an] infinite number of beautiful islands having on them very pleasant and delightful meadows and groves in which in spring and summer one sees a great number of birds which come there in their time and season.

Samuel de Champlain, on the islands of the St. Lawrence River, and in particular, Ile d'Orleans, just below Quebec City

✦

It is only here in large portions of Canada that wondrous *second wind*, the Indian summer, attains its amplitude and heavenly perfection—the temperatures, the sunny haze; the mellow, rich, delicate, almost *flavoured* air: "Enough to live —enough to merely be."

American poet **Walt Whitman** in 1880

✦

I knew nothing finer, either from the point of view of the sociologist, the traveller, or the artist, than a month's devotion to even the surface of Canada, over the line of the Great Lakes and the St. Lawrence, the fertile, populous, and happy province of Ontario, the province of Quebec, with another month to the hardy maritime regions of New Brunswick, Nova Scotia and Newfoundland.

Walt Whitman in 1880

I see, or imagine I see in the future, a race of two million farm-families, ten million people—every farm running down to the water, or at least in sight of it—the best air and drink and sky and scenery of the globe, the sure foundation-nutriment of heroic men and women. The summers, the winters —I have sometimes doubted whether there could be a great race without the hardy influence of winters in due proportion.

Walt Whitman, from *Walt Whitman's Diary in Canada*, 1904

❀

I must say, however, that though Florida may have a more favourable climate than anything I've seen and its soil may be more fruitful, you could hardly hope to find a more beautiful country than Canada.

Samuel de Champlain in 1603

❀

You feare the *Winters* cold, sharp, piercing ayre
They love it best, that have once wintered here.

Robert Hayman, former governor of the Bristol, Eng. merchants' plantation at Conception Bay, Nfld., in 1628

❀

Every year they ask the sky to send down as much snow, hail and frost as it can contain. What they really need are Canadian or Russian winters. Their own nests will be all the warmer, all the downier, all the better loved.

French poet **Charles Baudelaire** (1821–67), on dreamers and visionaries

If vastness of plains, and magnitude of lake, mountain, and river can make a land as great, then no region posseses higher claims to that distinction.

William Francis Butler, Irish military and
intelligence officer, on Canada in *The Great
Lone Land*, 1872

❀

They told me, casually, that there was nothing but a few villages between me and the North Pole ... it gives me a thrill to hear it.

English poet **Rupert Brooke** in 1916

❀

Unseizable virginity.

Rupert Brooke on Canada

❀

There is a vigor and strength in the Canadian spring as in no other country in the world.

Blaise Cendrars (1887–1961), French art critic,
poet, novelist and filmmaker

❀

Canada has fascinated me since childhood. As a boy in Ireland, I was intrigued by the sporting trophies my father brought home from there—moose heads, bear and buffalo rugs, Indian bows and arrows, not to mention three black bear cubs and a young elk stag, all very much alive.

Earl Alexander of Tunis, governor-general of
Canada 1946–52, in 1969

It is impossible to describe the country, for it is built on a scale outside that of humanity.

> British author and parliamentarian **John Buchan**, Lord Tweedsmuir, governor-general of Canada 1935–40, in a 1935 reference to Fort Providence on Great Slave Lake

❦

I think British Columbia very like heaven, or like what I should like my heaven to be, if ever I arrive so high—one mass of mountains, with mirrors of water mixed with them, torrents and forests, and roaring Rhones.

> British novelist **M. P. Shiel** in 1935

❦

October is the loveliest Canadian month. For some time frosts have been stealing down at night from the north and forcing that sad crisis in the woods—the death of the leaves. Nothing in Nature is more memorable than the transformation which then takes place. The funeral rites of the Canadian trees are celebrated with pageantry of startling gorgeousness. Gradually the dark, sultry green of the summer foliage is changed into many lighter, gayer, more vivid hues. Each day the wonder grows until in the first half of October it reaches its climax.

> British High Commissioner **Malcolm MacDonald** in 1947

❦

The arctic expresses the sum total of all wisdom: Silence. Nothing but silence. The end of time.

> German poet **Walter Bauer** in 1968

Canada is horizontal. Only a comparatively narrow strip above the American border is populated. Like a layer of cream on a jug of milk … a strip of earth and an expanse of sky. The sky is ever sensed above Canada, untamed nature to the pole —green sky of summer and white of winter.

Russian writer **Andrei Voznesensky** in 1971

❦

Outside Calgary, we drove up into the Rockies. Finally we had crossed the plains. Now as we ran down the last miles into British Columbia it was as if nature ran riot after the almost existential bleakness of the prairies; the lushness and size of everything we saw seemed preposterously exaggerated. Our spirits lifted with the beauty of the place and its lush vegetation, huge waterfalls, deep black fjords and massive dark green pine forests.

Rock musician **Bob Geldof** in 1973,
impressions during a bus trip from
Montreal to Vancouver

❦

To say that Western Canada is one of the most magnificent regions of North America is not a trite superlative but an understatement. Within this vast region are some of the highest mountains on the North American continent; sprawling glaciers and giant trees; scores of wild rivers and thousands of unnamed lakes; seacoasts, richly described in Indian legend; sprawling prairies thick with golden wheat; and the mysterious Arctic region, itself inhabited by the "first people" of the Western Hemisphere. One will also find cosmopolitan cities … Western Canada is an untamed wilderness that also offers the utmost in human civilization.

U.S. travel writer **Frederick Pratson** in 1987

There is a fifth coast of North America, one that lies not at the edge like the other four, not along the Atlantic or the Pacific or the Caribbean or the ice-swept, lonely Arctic, but at the centre, along the midcontinental line. It is a spectacular coast.

U.S. environmentalist **William Ashworth** in 1986,
on the Great Lakes

❧

Throughout my childhood, Canada was always perceived as a more beautiful, unspoiled version of New Hampshire and Maine. We certainly had—I think most Americans had—no sense of any nationalistic differences.

U.S. novelist **John Irving** in 1990

❧

From the air, the [Magdalen] islands look like fragile strands of sand flung across the sea ... Inviting beaches, in tints of pink and tan and edged with blue-green waters, stretch for miles. Bright red sandstone cliffs erode, constantly replenishing dunes and beaches ... After sand, the first thing that impresses you in the Magdalens is the brightly coloured houses. A rainbow of house paint scatters across the landscape: intense robin's-egg blue, periwinkle, apple green, forest green, persimmon, yellow, deep purple. The taste for vivid colours, some say, came with the Acadians, from whom most of the 15,000 islanders are descended.

U.S. writer **Jennifer C. Urquhart** in 1991

Everyone who comes to Labrador talks about the beauty of this country, the wilderness aspect. Canoeists and kayakers view it as pristine. But let me tell you, there's no place here that native people haven't been—and left marks to prove it. Maybe not on the highest peaks. But they've been up, down, and around most of the mountains and everywhere else.

University of South Carolina archaeologist **Stephen Loring** in 1991, noting that Newfoundland and Labrador's wild, unpopulated image contrasts with its history as a centuries-old crossroads of explorers and settlers

ENCHANTED PLACES

July 2: A beautiful day for Labrador. Went on shore, and was most pleased with what I saw. The country, so wild and grand, is of itself enough to interest anyone in its wonderful dreariness.

U.S. naturalist **John James Audubon**, 1833
diary entry

✿

Newfoundland has special claims upon us, for though sentiment is generally out of place in politics, it cannot be forgotten that Newfoundland is England's first born. That foggy little island, although perhaps somewhat of a rough diamond, is a valuable jewel.

Irish statesman **Earl of Dunraven** in 1914

✿

Beloved Island.

U.S. President **Franklin Roosevelt**'s name for
the Roosevelt family retreat at Campobello
Island, N.B.

Much as we may admire the various bays, and lakes, and inlets, promontories, and straits, the mountains and woodlands of this rarely-visited corner of creation—and, compared with it, we [Americans] can boast of no scenery so beautiful—the valley of Grand Pre transcends all the rest in the Province. Only our valley of Wyoming, as an inland picture, may match it, both in beauty and tradition.

> American essayist **Frederick Swartwout Cozzens**, on a 1856 tour of Acadian settlements in Nova Scotia

❖

I have travelled around the globe. I have seen the Canadian and the American Rockies, the Andes and the Alps and the Highlands of Scotland; but for simple beauty, Cape Breton Island outrivals them all.

> Edinburgh-born American inventor **Alexander Graham Bell**, sometime resident of Cape Breton Island

❖

Among my fondest memories—from childhood to the present—are those summers I spent in Baddeck, N.S., at the house built by my great-grandfather Alexander Graham Bell … The Bras d'Or Lake region has changed little since I was a small child. It still possesses the physical beauty that drew my ancestors there in the nineteenth century. And today, my children are the fifth generation of our family to sail the pristine waters near Baddeck.

> **Gilbert M. Grosvenor**, president of the Washington, D.C.-based National Geographic Society, in 1991

It is a neat and well-kept province almost entirely lacking the huge hoardings and other such signs of North American life. Instead, its landscapes are a kaleidoscope of colours: blue sea, red sand, green trees and crops, red soil and above them on fine days a blue sky with puffy white clouds.

Michelin Guide to Canada on Prince Edward Island, 1985

❀

Sydney [N.S.] is a pleasant rural picture. Everybody has heard of the Sydney coal-mines: we expected to find the miner's finger-marks everywhere; but instead of the smoky, sulphurous atmosphere, and the black road, and the sulky, grimy, brick tenements, we were surprised with clean, white, picket-fences; and green lawns, and clever, little cottages, nestled in shrubbery and clover.

Frederick Swartwout Cozzens in 1856

❀

My lifelong dream came true today.

Haruko Hakada, 28, of Sendai, Japan, in 1995, on her marriage at Cavendish, P.E.I. as part of a $3,300 deluxe wedding tour package in which couples re-enact Anne Shirley's marriage ceremony in *Anne of Green Gables*. For those who cannot afford to be among the 15,000 Japanese women and young couples to visit P.E.I. each year, Anne-style weddings are a feature of Canadian World on the Japanese island of Hokkaido, the world's first theme park dedicated to aspects of Canadian life, billed by its promoters as a project "intended to bring to life the sense of romance,

exoticism and nostalgia implicit [in]
Canada's nineteenth-century rural scenes,
towns and the great outdoors."

✦

Oh, the air! You know what it is when we land at Dieppe, or at
Brussels, or Aix. Well, all that air is fog, depressing wet blan-
ket compared to this Canadian nectar. I really doubt whether
it would not be almost worth while to emigrate merely for
the exquisite pleasure of the act of living in this country.
English novelist **Thomas Hughes**, on an 1870
visit to Quebec

✦

In spite of jails on the one side and convents on the other
and the thin black wreck of the Quebec Railway Bridge, lying
like a dumped carload of tin cans in the river, the Eastern
Gate to Canada is noble with a dignity beyond words.
English writer **Rudyard Kipling**, on a Quebec
City visit in 1908, one year after a tragedy in
which the Quebec Bridge's southern span
fell into the St. Lawrence River during
construction, killing 75 workmen

✦

The stupendous Quebec countryside: At the point of Diamond
Cape before the immense breach of the Saint Lawrence, air,
light, and water interpenetrate in infinite proportions. For the
first time on this continent, a real impression of beauty and
true magnitude.
French writer **Albert Camus**, on an 1946 trip
to New York and Montreal

Beyond [the Gaspé north coast town of] Tadoussac, country-and-western music blasted earnestly on the car radio—as twangy in French as in English—*"Toujours dans mon coeur*—Always in my heart"* ... The stark beauty of the place—the wildness, the surf-battered rocks, the clean-lined churches —will remain with me. And the cheerful warmth of the people that comes in a hundred ways—a gift of strawberries, the sharing of tea and cakes, a pot of steaming mussels around a kitchen table—these will stay, in the words of the country song, *toujours dans mon coeur.*

Jennifer C. Urquhart in 1991

❧

The beauty of this noble stream at almost any point, but especially in the commencement of this journey when it winds its way among the Thousand Islands, can hardly be imagined. The number and constant successions of these islands, all green and richly wooded; their fluctuating sizes, some so large that for half an hour together one among them will appear as the opposite bank of the river, and some so small that they are mere dimples on its broad bosom; their infinite variety of shapes; and the numberless combinations of beautiful forms which the trees growing on them present: all form a picture fraught with uncommon interest and pleasure.

Charles Dickens in his 1842 memoir
American Notes

Here the landscape is one of the most beautiful in North America. The immense sheet of the lake is of an almost white blue shade. Hundreds and hundreds of small green islands float on the calm surface of limpid waters. The delightful cottages built in brightly coloured bricks make that landscape look like an enchanted kingdom.

Blaise Cendrars, on a visit to the
Thousand Islands

❧

As we neared Point Levi, opposite Quebec, we got our first view of the St. Lawrence. "Iliad of rivers!" exclaimed my friend. "Yet unsung!"

The Hudson must take a back seat now, and a good way back. One of the two or three great water-courses of the globe is before you. No other river, I imagine, carries such a volume of pure cold water to the sea … The great lakes are its camping grounds; here its hosts repose under the sun and stars in areas like that of states and kingdoms, and it is its waters that shake the earth at Niagara. Where it receives the Saguenay it is twenty miles wide, and when in debouches into the Gulf it is a hundred. Indeed, it is a chain of Homeric sublimities from beginning to end. The great cataract is a fit sequel to the great lakes; the spirit that is born in vast and tempestuous Superior takes its full glut of power in that fearful chasm. If paradise is hinted at in the Thousand Islands, hell is unveiled in that pit of horrors.

American essayist **John Burroughs**, in his 1877
essay "Halcyon in Canada"

Niagara!
Thou with thy rushing waters dost restore
The heavenly gift that sorrow took away.

> Cuban author **Jose Maria Heredia**, in his
> 1827 poem "Niagara"

❦

When the beholder has stood awhile, and perceives no lull in
the storm, and considers that the vapor and the foam are as
everlasting as the rocks which produce them, all this turmoil
assumes a sort of calmness. It soothes while it awes the mind.

> American novelist **Nathaniel Hawthorne** in an
> 1832 account of his impression on viewing
> the Canadian falls at Niagara

❦

I have seen it (Niagara) yet live ... My mind whirled off, it
seemed to me, in a strange world. It seemed unearthly, like
the strange, dim images in the Revelation. I thought of the
great white throne; the rainbow around it; the throne in sight
like unto an emerald; and oh! that beautiful water rising like
moonlight, falling as the soul sinks when it dies, to rise refined,
spiritualized, and pure.

> American novelist **Harriet Beecher Stowe**,
> impressions of Niagara Falls during
> a 1834 visit

❦

It drives me frantic with excitement.

> American poet **Henry Wadsworth Longfellow** on a
> 1862 visit to Niagara Falls

We sat down opposite the American Falls, finding them the first day or two more level to our comprehension than the Great Horseshoe Cataract; yet throughout, the beauty was far more impressive to me than the grandeur. One's imagination may heap up almost any degree of grandeur; but the subtle colouring of this scene, varying with every breath of wind refining upon the softness of driven snow, and dimming all the gems of mine, is wholly inconceivable.

English novelist **Harriet Martineau**, impressions from a 1836 visit to Niagara Falls

♦

Hurried to the Horse-shoe fall. I went down alone, into the very basin. It would be hard for a man to stand nearer to God than he does here. There was a bright rainbow at my feet; and from that I looked up—great Heaven! to what a fall of bright green water! The broad, deep, mighty stream seems to die in the act of falling; and, from its unfathomable grave arises that tremendous ghost of spray which is never laid, and has been haunting this place with the same dread solemnity —perhaps from the creation of the world ... To say anything about this wonderful place, would be sheer nonsense. It far exceeds my most sanguine expectations—although the impression on my mind has been, from the first, nothing but Beauty and Peace.

Charles Dickens on a 1842 visit to Niagara Falls

♦

The prettiest Sunday afternoon drive in the world.

Winston Churchill after a motor trip on the Niagara Parkway in 1943

You purchase release at last by the fury of your indifference, and stand there gazing your fill at the most beautiful object in the world. The perfect taste of it is the great characteristic. It is not in the least monstrous; it is thoroughly artistic and, as the phrase is, thought out. In the matter of line it beats Michael Angelo ... The genius who invented it was certainly the first author of the idea that order, proportion and symmetry are the conditions of perfect beauty. He applied his faith among the watching and listening forests, long before the Greeks proclaimed theirs in the measurements of the Parthenon.

> American novelist **Henry James** in an 1883 travelogue, on an 1871 visit to Niagara Falls

✤

The story within a story is an honoured technique of literature and film. The Stratford Festival is in a sense theatre within theatre, for it offers great repertory theatre set in a thriving community. The visitor may often find it difficult to know where the theatre stops and the workaday world begins. After all, isn't the Shakespearean Gardens, containing the range of herbs mentioned in the Bard's work, or the panache of the chef and staff at Rundles, or the murmuring course of the river through town as much a matter of theatre as the lines of the plays themselves?

> U.S. broadcaster **Gene Burns** in an *Atlantic Monthly* travel story on Stratford, Ontario, in 1994

It has the merit, from the shore, of producing a slight ambi-
guity of vision. It is the sea, and yet just not the sea. The huge
expanse, the landless line of the horizon, suggest the ocean;
while an indefinable shortness of pulse, a kind of fresh-water
gentleness of tone, seem to contradict the idea.

Henry James in 1883, describing Lake Ontario

❧

If I had not exhausted all my superlatives of delight, I
could be eloquent on the charms of this exquisite little lake
[Couchiching], and the wild beauty of the rapids … This
most beautiful piece of water [Lake Superior] is above forty
miles in length, and about twenty in breadth, and is in winter so firmly frozen over, that it is crossed in sledges in every
direction.

Dublin-born writer **Anna Jameson**, from *Winter
Studies and Summer Rambles in Canada,*
an account of her nine-month sojourn in
Canada, 1836–37

❧

We were certainly very happy in our fairyland of peace and
loveliness amid the Muskoka Lakes of Northern Ontario …
The Muskoka interlude remained for me a sparkling, radiant
memory, alight with the sunshine of unclouded skies, with
the gleam of stars in a blue-black heaven, swept by forest
winds, and set against a background of primeval forests that
stretched without a break for six hundred miles of lonely and
untrodden beauty.

British mystery and travel writer **Algernon
Blackwood** (1869–1951), from his memoirs

The Canadian Shield—a vast, mineral-rich region that covers half of Canada. Ahead of us stretched a watery world: Glorious lakes, big and small, spangle much of Ontario, as well as Manitoba, northern Saskatchewan and Alberta, and the Northwest Territories … Once you're bitten by Canada's north woods (and the mosquitoes and black flies will bite you, never fear), you must go back. And once you've seen the Muskokas, you must go on, northwest to Wawa, Norway House, The Pas, and Flin Flon.

U.S. writer and editor Ralph Gray, in 1967

❦

Do you know, when the Millerites over in Buffalo prophesied that the world was going to come to an end on a certain day, do you know what they did? They hiked over to Canada! Now, I sympathize with the move and with the proceding. My heart is in Canada, part of it, and I have bought a little farm not long ago—out there in Saskatchewan, I like it so much, I like to have a little Canadian real estate.

Elbert Hubbard in a 1911 Toronto speech

❦

The air is different from any air that ever blew, the space is ampler than most spaces, because it runs back to the unhampered Pole, and the open land keeps the secret of its magic as closely as the sea or the desert. People here do not stumble against each other around corners, but see largely and tranquilly from a long way off what they desire, or wish to avoid, and they shape their path accordingly across the waves, and troughs, and tongues, and dips and fans of the land.

Rudyard Kipling on the Canadian Prairies,
in 1908

I thought I hated the prairie through the long winter months, and yet somehow it has caught hold of me. It was dreary and monotonous, and yet I can't get it out of my heart. There's a beauty and a romance in it which fill my soul with longing.

British novelist **Somerset Maugham** in *The Land of Promise*, a three-act play written in 1912

❋

On impulse I bought a four-thousand-acre ranch ... in the valley of the Highwood River, some forty miles south of Calgary ... My impulse in making this investment—the only piece of property that I have ever owned—was far removed from Imperial politics. In the midst of that irresistible countryside I had suddenly been overwhelmed by an irresistible longing to immerse myself, if only momentarily, in the simple life of the Western prairies. There, I was sure, I would find occasional escape from the sometimes too-confining, too well-ordered, island life of Great Britain.

Edward VIII in his 1951 memoirs. As Duke of Windsor, Edward visited Canada four times between 1919 and 1927; he renounced the British throne in 1936

❋

The great plains of northern Canada are wide and flat, endless pine forest and corn prairie, corn prairie and pine forest, through which the roads, straight as knives, run on seemingly forever; wonderful roads they are for cycling, though you seldom see a cyclist on them.

English author **Joan Aiken** in 1972

Saskatchewan is much like Texas—except it's more friendly to the United States.

U.S. statesman **Adlai Stevenson**

❋

We spent the morning in a buggy going out to see a lake called Emerald Lake. It is a wonderful splendid deep emerald green. Enormous mountains capped with snow and covered with pine stand all round it and their reflections in the water are all tinted green. I thought to myself and Mummy thought so too that after a few years, if all goes well, you and [your sister] will have a month's camping with us in this wonderful land.

Rudyard Kipling, during a 1907 visit to Mount Stephen House, in the Rockies near present-day Field, B.C.

❋

Jasper Park is one of the great national playgrounds and health resorts which the Canadian Government with great wisdom has laid out for the benefit of its citizens. When Canada has filled up and carries a large population, she will bless the foresight of the administrators who took possession of broad tracts of the most picturesque land and put them for ever out of the power of the speculative dealer. The National Park at Banff has for twenty years been a Mecca for tourists. That at Algonquin gives a great pleasure-ground to those who cannot extend their travels beyond Eastern Canada.

British physician and detective-story writer **Arthur Conan Doyle**, on a 1914 tour of the Rockies

I've nothing to tell you, except that the mountains are ... and the lake is ... and the snow and trees are ... but it would take me weeks to get out what they are, and I haven't time, for I want this letter to go today or tomorrow. Suffice it that they are wonderful.

British writer **Rupert Brooke** in a 1913 letter to a friend, posted from Lake Louise, Alberta

❧

My old familiar Rockies! Have I been here before? What an absurd question, when I lived here for about ten years of my life in all the hours of dreamland. What deeds have I not done among Redskins and trappers and grizzlies within their wilds! And here they were at last glimmering bright in the rising morning sun.... I have seen my dream mountains. Most boys never do.

Arthur Conan Doyle in 1914

❧

Earth, it seemed, was at peace.

And I, looking over all that vastness of life, felt my own greatness thrust upon me.

For had not the Creator of all things made this wonderful place for *me*?

American novelist **James Oliver Curwood** on the Rockies, in his 1921 autobiography *God's Country: The Trail to Happiness*

❧

When I speak of the travellers who consider Stanley Park the most beautiful of all, emphatically, among them I number myself.

Welsh travel writer **Jan Morris** in 1968

On three sides of me spread out the wonderful panorama of the Canadian Rockies, softened in the golden sunshine of late June. From up and down the valley, from the breaks between the peaks, and from the little gullies cleft in shale and rock that crept up to the snow-lines came a soft and droning murmur. It was the music of running water—music ever in the air of summer, for the rivers and creeks and tiny streamlets gushing down from the melting snow up near the clouds are never still.

James Oliver Curwood in 1921

❦

We went to the Rockies, to Lake Louise and Banff. Lake Louise was for a long time my answer when I was asked which was the most beautiful place I had ever seen:—a great, long, blue lake, low mountains on either side, all of a most glorious shape, closing in with snow mountains at the end of it.

British mystery writer **Agatha Christie**, during a 1922 trip to Canada

❦

To describe the beauties of this region will, on some future occasion, be a very grateful task to the pen of a skilled panegyrist. The serenity of the climate, the innumerable pleasing landscapes, and the abundant fertility that unassisted nature puts forth, requires only to be enriched by the industry of man with villages, mansions, cottages, and other buildings to render it the most lovely country that can be imagined.

Captain **George Vancouver**, description of the site of present-day Vancouver, in 1792

Saltspring Island … lured there by an observation by Malcolm Lowry to the effect that in the islands off Vancouver the twentieth century seemed more remote than anywhere else in the world. Lowry's opinion proved to be correct, and I would gladly have stayed on the island to the end of my days if it had been practicable—which it isn't.

British author Malcolm Muggeridge in 1979

*

The forest was magnificent, the richest, greenest, most verdant I had ever seen. The cedars and firs, massive and straight, stood far apart, and towered over the jungle of underbrush which consisted largely of broad-leaved maples. It seemed impenetrable. How wet and glistening with darkly green! This was a country of rain, of fertility. Vines and creepers matted the underbrush. In the heart of this woodland, a few miles up from the settlement, the Campbell River plunged into a canyon, making a waterfall that matched the surroundings.

American author Zane Grey, on a 1919 fishing
trip to Campbell River, B.C.

*

At the remote southern end of the Queen Charlotte Islands, an archipelago some 60 miles west of Prince Rupert, there's not much that reminds you of the twentieth century. There are no power lines, no chain saws, no gas stations or other facilities in the verdant wilderness of 138 islands called South Moresby. Unique life-forms—rare flowering plants, the smallest saw-whet owls, the largest black bears in Canada, and species of birds, shrews, and mosses found nowhere else —make this misty, storm-lashed fragment of the country's western shores a naturalist's dream.

U.S. writer Cynthia Ross Ramsay in 1991

The maze of waterways, with twisting straits and inlets, has made the B.C. coast a paradise for sailors, kayakers, and other boaters. The coastal seas sustain one of the world's great commercial fisheries, teeming with halibut, cod, herring, and five species of Pacific salmon—coho, king, sockeye, pink and chum. To these bountiful waters tens of thousands of people come each year to fish, casting for the "smileys," the big ones anglers dream about.

Cynthia Ross Ramsay in 1991

＊

British Columbia may be beset by problems, economic and political, but it's an enjoyable corner of the world, far from the Presbyterian restraints of Ontario and the climate constraints of the rest of Canada. Its residents, though accused of aping Californians, secretly aspire to be Tahitians.

English travel writer **Stephen Brook** in 1987

＊

There are few places left on the North American continent where men can still see the country as it was before Europeans came and know some of the challenges and freedoms of those who saw it first, but in the Canadian Northwest it can still be done.

Minnesota naturalist **Sigurd F. Olson** in 1961

＊

The great elements of Fire and Earth, Air and Water still hold sway, if not untrammeled, in the wild Rocky Mountains and north to the Arctic in the land of the Nahanni, "somewhere over there and beyond."

Ranulph Fiennes in 1973. Fiennes, a Briton, led an expedition from the Arctic Circle through the B.C. Interior to Vancouver in 1971

The notion that the Arctic climate, notorious for its severe windchill, prolonged dark winters, and freezing temperatures for much of the year, could support an abundance of wildlife seems at first glance rather hallucinatory. I scanned my surroundings at the seal hole and saw a desert ... As with every desert, however, there are oases, and few are more fabulous, more extravagant with life, than the Arctic floe edge, where landfast ice ends and open water begins. During the bright season between May and July, the receding ice becomes a platform from which one can watch along the nearby waters an unbelievable stream of migratory birds and marine mammals moving into the high latitudes to breed and feed.

U.S. writer **Thomas O'Neill** in 1991, on a tour of
Baffin Island in the Northwest Territories

◆

Among the Canadian rivers I've seen—and there have been some wild ones—none is so treacherous as the South Nahanni ... After two days and 120 miles of rough going, we rounded a bend in a winding canyon, heard the boom of a cataract, and looked directly into a wall of water, water to the skyline! We had reached Virginia Falls, the continent's most pristine, remote, and fabulous waterfall. Estimates vary as to whether Canada contains one-third or one-fourth of the world's fresh water, but it seemed that all of it was pouring down in front of me, a sense-shattered curtain 316 feet high. I thought of Albert Faille, Raymond M. Patterson, John Lentz, and the other adventurers who had reached this spot before me. But while I watched, I felt that this waterfall was mine.

U.S. adventurer **Richard W. Montague** in 1967, on
a boat trip down the Northwest Territories'
South Nahanni river

THE PEOPLE

We felt that we were at home, and everywhere we were received like compatriots, children of Old France, as they say here. To my mind the epithet is badly chosen. Old France is in Canada, the new is with us.

French writer **Alexis de Tocqueville**, on an 1831 visit to Quebec

❦

French Canadians are a separate people in America, a people of a distinct and vivacious national character, a new and healthy people whose origins are entirely warlike, with its language, its religion, its laws, its customs, a nation more densely populated than any other of the new world; which could be conquered but not dissolved by force to be absorbed into the milieu of the Anglo American race.

Alexis de Tocqueville in an 1838 letter to his British translator, commenting on the recent rebellions of 1837 in both Upper and Lower Canada

Canadian girls are so pretty it is a relief to see a plain one now and then.

> American writer **Mark Twain** on a Montreal
> trip in 1881

＊

Etiquette may perhaps be defined as some rule of social conduct. I have found that no such rule is necessary in Canada, for the self-respect of the people guarantees good manners.

> Governor General **Marquis of Lorne** in 1883

＊

The French, it is true, were unable to maintain this magnificent American colony; but the population, the great majority of it, did not become less French, but bound itself to ancient Gaul by those ties of blood, that racial identity, those natural instincts that international politics never managed to break.

In reality, the "few acres of snow," as they were so disdainfully dismissed, form a kingdom the surface of which is equal to that of Europe.

> French writer **Jules Verne** in a novel, *Les
> voyages extraordinaires*, published in
> Paris in the 1890s

＊

I don't think the spirit of Rationalism has touched them at all. They … have no thoughts on unpleasant subjects of the soul but follow their good bishop and go to church and sing, oh sing, hymns on all occasions possible … It is quite refreshing to be among them.

> **Douglas Hyde**, future president of Ireland, on
> the citizenry of Fredericton, where he taught
> Modern Languages at the University of
> New Brunswick in 1890–91

In Russia, in the northern parts of the United States, the people say: "It's too cold to go out." In Canada, they say: "It's very cold, let's all go out" … The driver wraps you up in furs, and as you go, gliding on the snow, your face is whipped by the cold air; you feel glowing all over with warmth, and altogether the sensation is delightful.

French travel writer **Paul Blouet** in his 1891 travel memoir *A Frenchman in America*

❦

Canada is essentially a country of the larger air, where men can still face the old primeval forces of Nature and be braced into vigour, and withal so beautiful that it can readily inspire that romantic patriotism which is one of the most priceless assets of a people.

John Buchan, Lord Tweedsmuir

❦

What a kind-hearted race of people are these Canadians! Here was I, an entire stranger among them, and yet every hour people were making enquiries, and interesting themselves on my behalf, bringing and sending books, grapes, bananas, and other delicacies for a sick man. When a second operation was deemed necessary, the leg had to be amputated at the knee, the whole town was concerned, and the doctors had to give strict injunctions not to admit such a number of kind-hearted visitors.

Welsh poet and author **William Henry Davies** (1871–1940), in his *The Autobiography of a Super-Tramp*, describing the aftermath of an accident he suffered while trying to hitch a ride on a train near Renfrew, Ont.

For the first time I met a people whose job was not to manage what already existed, but to develop it without stint. No
one thought about limits; no one knew where the frontier was.

French statesman **Jean Monnet**, founder of the
European Economic Community, impressions
from a 1906 stint as a salesman travelling in
Winnipeg and Calgary

❖

In Germany we honour all heroes—no matter their nationality. In the pages of Germany's History of the Great War,
General Currie is mentioned as the greatest General the war
produced. Had it not been for you Canadians, and the far-
seeing tactics of Sir Arthur Currie, victory would most certainly have been ours.

German officer quoted in **Daniel G. Dancocks'**
1985 biography, Sir Arthur Currie. Canadian
victories in First World War action, notably at
Vimy Ridge and Passchendaele, won an
unusual tribute in *Der Weltkrieg 1914–18*, the
German official war history, which refers to
the "obstinate resistance" and "tenacious
determination" of Canadian troops, and
prompted a German war correspondent
to report in a 1918 despatch that the
"Canadians are much the best troops that
the English have." In 1918, Currie himself, in
congratulating his Canadian Corps troops,
noted that in only two months they had
"encountered and defeated decisively 47
German divisions—that is nearly a quarter of
the German forces on the Western Front."

Whenever the Germans found the Canadian Corps coming into the line, they prepared for the worst.

> **David Lloyd George**, British prime minister during the First World War, in his memoirs

❦

Surprising as it may be to many Canadians, the average American is tremendously proud of Canada's war record. An American who served with the Canadian forces, whether in the A.S.C. or originals, is a hero to his fellow countrymen.

> American novelist **Ernest Hemingway** in a 1920 *Star Weekly* article

❦

When I first took command of the Canadian forces, someone said to me, "For goodness sake, never patronize the Canadians," to which I replied, "By Heaven, I would as soon patronize a wasp's nest."

> Governor-General **Lord Byng of Vimy** in 1921

❦

There they stood on Vimy Ridge that 9th day of April 1917, men from Quebec stood shoulder to shoulder with men from Ontario, men from the Maritimes with men from British Columbia, and there was forged a nation tempered by the fires of sacrifice and hammered on the anvil of high adventure.

> **Lord Byng of Vimy** in a 1922 tribute to Canadian Corps troops

❦

May I offer one or two suggestions to you in Canada, especially in Ontario? Go ahead and keep your lead with regard to all that encourages the home life of your people.

> Salvation Army leader **Bramwell Booth** in a 1913 Toronto address

I do want to take my hat off once again to the French Canadian. He came of a small people. At the time of the British occupation, I doubt if there were more than a hundred thousand of them, and yet the mark they have left by their bravery and activity upon this continent is an ineffaceable one ... They were more than scouts in the army. They were so far ahead that the army will take a century yet before it reaches their outposts. Brave, enduring, lighthearted, romantic, they were and are a fascinating race. The ideals of the British and of the French stock may not be the same, but while the future of the country must surely be upon British lines, the French will leave their mark deeply upon it ... It seems to me that the British cannot be too dedicated in their dealings with such a people. They are not a subject people but partners in empire, and should in all ways be treated so.

Arthur Conan Doyle, writing in the *Cornhill Magazine*, after a 1914 visit to Canada, during which he spent time in Montreal, Winnipeg, Edmonton, Algonquin Park and Ottawa

❦

Chicago calls Toronto a puritan town.
But both boxing and horse-racing are illegal in Chicago ...
If you kill somebody with a motor car in Ontario
You are liable to go to jail.
So it isn't done.
There have been over 500 people killed by motor cars
In Chicago so far this year.

Ernest Hemingway, in a 1924 poem, "I Like Canadians"

"And bring your friend," said Mrs. Braddocks, laughing. She was a Canadian and had all their easy social graces.

Ernest Hemingway, *The Sun Also Rises*, 1926

❦

It is indeed a mosaic of vast dimensions and great breadth.

U.S. travel writer **Victoria Hayward** in 1922, on the ethnic diversity of the Prairies

❦

The Nova Scotians keep the Sabbath. They do not fish on the seventh day of the week. I am afraid they made me feel ashamed of my own lack of reverence. More and more we Americans drift away from the Church and its influence. Perhaps that is another reason for our lawlessness, our waning home life, our vanishing America ... Liverpool [N.S.] was to awaken in me something long buried under the pagan self-absorption of life in the United States ... I shall respect the custom of the Nova Scotians and stay quietly in the hotel on that day.

Zane Grey on a 1924 tuna-fishing expedition in Nova Scotia

❦

They are the best-tempered, best-mannered people walking. I do not believe I ever heard a Newfoundlander swear ... they are gay, good-humoured and generous; tolerant, temperate, tough, God-fearing, sabbath-keeping and law-abiding ... they will subscribe the earth for a man who had fallen through a rickety bridge, but do nothing at all about mending the bridge.

A. P. Herbert, British humorist and M.P., in 1943

This trip gave me a glimpse of Canada, an impression of its immensity and diversity, and the chance to meet many kind and congenial people who have become lifelong friends. I left Canada thrilled with what I had seen, eager to return and to be somehow, at some time and in some place, a participant in the adventure of developing this land with its vast possibilities, so many of them still dormant, still undreamed —the romance of Canada.

> Irish director **Tyrone Guthrie**, future
> founding artistic director of the Stratford
> Shakespearean Festival, during his first
> visit to Canada, in 1929

❦

Vancouver. My head is in a whirl. My thoughts were playing leapfrog. I was free! Who was it once said that only those who have been slaves can understand freedom? It seemed to me, walking through the main streets with a group of my shipmates, that I had never before seen so many relaxed, unafraid, happy people in one place at one time.

> Soviet engineer **Victor Kravchenko** in 1943, who
> defected to the West eight months after his
> North American trip

❦

Between my country and Canada lie a great sea and a mighty ocean, yet our countries are close to one another, because Turks and Canadians have this in common: the love of life; the desire to live a little better day by day; the hope of the joy of neither killing nor dying for the sake of foul imperialist profits.

> Turkish poet **Nazim Hikmet** in 1951

"It's something my people haven't got. Or if we have got it, it all happened long ago across the water and so now there ain't nothing to look at every day to remind us of it. We don't live among defeated grandfathers and freed slaves … and bullets in the dining room table and such, to be always reminding us to never forget."

Shreve McCannon, an Albertan, explains to his Harvard University dorm-mate Quentin Compson, who is from Jefferson, Miss., why he can't comprehend the violent, racially convoluted history of the American South, in **William Faulkner**'s *Absalom! Absalom!* (1936)

❀

If the future of mankind in a unified world is going to be on the whole a happy one, then I would prophesy that there is a future in the Old World for the Chinese, and in the island of North America for the Canadiens. Whatever the future of mankind in North America, I feel pretty confident that these French-speaking Canadians, at any rate, will be there at the end of the story.

British historian **Arnold Toynbee** in 1948

❀

Canada. What a beautiful country. The air and the sky seem to have been freshly washed and polished, and the people too. Like the Swedes, the Canadians have un-northern temperments. Such capacity for enthusiasm!

Actress **Marlene Dietrich** in 1961

It's doubtful if the British can, any more than anyone else, see themselves as others see them. However, it is generally conceded that Canadians can see both Britain and the United States in clearer perspective than either can see the other.

Actor **Douglas Fairbanks, Jr.** in 1965

✤

I personally like Canadians. Very business-like people. They know what they want, which is no mean achievement. And they are proceeding towards their goal boldly, courageously and that, too, is not just a simple thing to do.

Soviet Foreign Minister **Alexei Kosygin** in 1971

✤

I have felt that if America was the last best hope of earth, as it started out to be, then the West was the place where the worst mistakes might be avoided and the best of the promises paid off. The average Canadian feels the same way. He feels more moral than Americans, and he has a lot more faith in his country than most Americans can generate.

American novelist **Wallace Stegner**
(1909–93) in 1973

✤

They're about the only ones left who still believe in it all, the Canadians.

British mystery writer **John le Carré** in 1968

Though in the intervening long summers and winters I have wandered over many lands in many climes and lived among diverse races—black, brown, yellow, and white—I remain as convinced as I was twenty years ago that there is no country in the world as beautiful as Canada, and there are no people in the world nicer than the Canadians.

To me, coming back to Canada is like coming back to my spiritual home. Canada quickened in me the impulse to appreciate the best there is in life; the ability to perceive beauty in things that are beautiful; the ability to love people who are lovable. It was in Canada that the desire to write came upon me. It was in Canada that I first saw my name in print. I owe more to this country and its people than I can put into words.

Indian author **Khushwant Singh** (b. 1915) during a lecture at Expo '67 in Montreal, twenty years after his first visit to Canada

❦

The Canadians were truly objective. They were also reasonably understanding and tolerant. And resigned. They had done enough of this "peacekeeping" work across the world by now that they seemed to have developed a tradition in their Army about how to handle it.

American novelist **James Jones** in 1974, on the Canadian peacekeeping forces in Vietnam

❦

The Canadian people strike visitors as among the world's friendliest, the most open and reasonable and least dogmatic, and now among the most economically aggressive and imaginative.

New York Times Toronto bureau chief **Andrew H. Malcolm** in his 1985 book, *The Canadians*

I like it here, I like Canadians very much. There is something in the air here, or in Canadians that makes the place more attractive than the United States is now. It must be like the Republic was some fifty years ago, before things took a turn for the worse.

U.S. author **Edmund Wilson** in a conversation
with Canadian novelist Morley Callaghan

❦

During the War of 1812, which was basically a scrap between Britain and the United States over fur trading, the Americans marched into Ontario to pull the wretched inhabitants from under the British boot-heel. They were astounded to be met by a hail of gunfire, and retreated at speed. The event appears in every Canadian history book and not, so far as I know, in a single American one.

Simon Hoggart, Washington correspondent for
the London-based *Observer*

❦

While there is great wealth [in Canada], I detect quite a bit of the "Boston Cracked Shoe" approach to wealth in the upper reaches of Canadian society. There used to be in Boston a great virtue in wearing shoes that, although they were highly polished and well cared-for, were so old they were beginning to crack at the seams—hence, the Boston Cracked Shoe. At very posh Canadian dinner parties, you will see people arriving not in limousines—they seem to want to make a point of arriving in a Subaru hatchback or a Volkswagen. To this day, among people who consider themselves to be superior folk in Toronto, it is not really considered good form to show off your wealth. It is that Scottish modesty.

American writer **Tom Wolfe** in 1987

I am deeply moved by the warmth and courage of the Canadian people which I felt so strongly during my recent visit to your country. Your support of the struggle against apartheid restored me in my journey home and reassured me that many just people around the world are with us.

> Archibishop **Desmond Tutu** of South Africa, in a
> 1986 letter in *The Toronto Star*

＊

Nineteen years ago I discovered Cape Breton when I was looking for a place I could afford to take my kids in the summer. I took the map of Nova Scotia and drove to the place with the fewest roads. I figured it would be isolated and I was right. It was years before anyone in the community figured out that I was a celebrity. A couple of years ago I was visiting my neighbour, a farmer who has since passed away. I was in his kitchen buying some cheese. His wife had just bought a piano and she asked me if I would play. He said to her, "Don't ask him to play the piano. When I go to his house, he doesn't ask me to milk the cows." I thought that was one of the smartest things I had ever heard anyone say. And I didn't play that piano.

> U.S. composer **Philip Glass** in 1987

＊

Everybody who has enough coins can photocopy a book of even 700–800 pages. The patience of the Canadians is infinite: they can wait until I reach the 700th page before complaining.

> Italian novelist **Umberto Eco**, on his frequent
> visits to the Robarts Library at the University
> of Toronto, where he studied semiotics in
> 1979 and 1981

Canadians are crazy. On the deepest level, they're the most loyal people in the world. No matter how well [Canadian] actors do in the United States, you can call them and say, "They want you to shovel squirrel dirt in a movie in Canada." And they'll say, "It's for Canada, I'll be there." They love being Canadians.

> U.S. film director **Paul Mazursky** (*Bob and Carol and Ted and Alice*), quoted in the 1988 book *Entertaining Canadians: Canada's International Stars 1900–1988*

❀

We get 3,000 letters a week, a lot from Canada. One thing about Canadians, they don't mail me their electric bills and ask me to pay for them—like some Americans have—and don't send me dirty responses when I don't. I love that.

> U.S. television talk-show host **Oprah Winfrey** in 1991

❀

It was one of the war's ironies that while thousands of Americans fled north to Canada to escape the draft, Canadians went south to join the fighting. After they obtained visas, Canadian volunteers were allowed to join the U.S. military, which was hungry for recruits as the war escalated ... "The Canadians have never had the chance to heal. We want to give them the respect they should have had 25, 30 years ago" [says Vietnam veteran Ed Johnson of Michigan, who was among the U.S. veterans to build a $180,000 granite memorial in a Windsor, Ont. park dedicated to the estimated 40,000 people who signed up for Vietnam service in Canada].

> ***Wall Street Journal*** report in 1995

A sign in the parking lot of the Toronto airport proclaims a "kiss 'n' fly" zone. It's a symptom of the endemic niceness of people in Toronto that no one considers this an invitation to open a bordello; instead, passengers are dropped off there for an airport shuttle bus. In this city of three million people, citizens cross only at crosswalks, people share taxis with strangers and buses carry the apologetic sign "Sorry ... Out of Service."

New York Times report in 1995

❋

We've always made fun of ourselves [in the North] as being boring and bland ... [But] we see the South as reactionary...I feel, then, like being publicly proud of Northernness, and celebrating its civility and its long tradition of tolerance and of reticence ... The idea of dominating or bullying other people is especially unattractive to us. We believe in equality even to the point of believing in mediocrity—we think that everyone should have their chance ... Canada and the Northern part of the States is almost one country—no, not one country. But almost one culture, a Northern culture.

Garrison Keillor, host of the Minnesota-based public-radio show *A Prairie Home Companion*, on his decision to broadcast the live show from a Canadian location (Vancouver) for the first time, in 1996, for broadcast in Canada and the U.S.

BEST CITIES

St. John's, Newfoundland, the most entertaining town in North America ... suggesting to me sometimes a primitive San Francisco, sometimes Bergen in Norway, occasionally China, and often Ireland of long ago.

Welsh travel writer **Jan Morris**

*

The Bedford basin where I sailed is the most remarkable sea-bay I was ever in ... the most complete sailing ground for boats and small vessels that can be imagined, and is at the same time large and deep enough to hold the whole British navy.

American lawyer and novelist
Richard Henry Dana, Jr., in 1842

*

Never had I beheld anything so beautiful and magnificent as the site of the city of Quebec; none better could have been chosen for that which it must one day become—the capital of a great empire.

Comte de Frontenac, governor of
New France, in 1672

The tiny fishing villages of the Martimes are at their most beautiful near Halifax, the bustling capital of Nova Scotia ... whose metropolitan population of over 300,000 makes it three times the size of its nearest rival, New Brunswick's Saint John. This pre-eminence has been achieved since World War II, but long before then Halifax was a naval town par excellence, its harbour defining the character and economy of a city which rarely seemed to look inland.

British travel writers **Tim Jepson**, **Phil Lee** and **Tania Smith** in 1992

❦

The impression made upon the visitor by this Gibraltar of America: ... It is mainly in the prospects from the site of the Old Government House, and from the Citadel, that [Quebec's] surpassing beauty lies. The exquisite expanse of country, rich in field and forest, mountain-height and water, which lies stretched out before the view, with miles of Canadian villages, glancing in long white streaks, like veins along the landscape; the motley crowd of gables, roofs, and chimney tops in the old hilly town immediately at hand; the beautiful St. Lawrence sparkling and flashing in the sunlight; and the tiny ships below the rock from which you gaze, whose distant rigging looks like spiders' webs against the light, while casks and barrels on their decks dwindle into toys, and busy mariners become so many puppets; all this, framed by a sunken window in the fortress and looked at from the shadowed room within, forms one of the brightest and most enchanting pictures that the eye can rest upon.

Charles Dickens in 1842

The hills all round, as seen from our celebrated platform [the Dufferin Terrace, which skirts Quebec's Chateau Frontenac hotel], are of the most lovely autumn colours, and covered, as they are with red and orange trees, they really look like flames in the distance, or like gigantic flower-gardens; for our trees are quite as brilliant as your best flowers, and if you can imagine your conservatory magnified a million times, and spread over miles and miles of hill and dale, you will begin to understand how we do things in [Canada].

Lady Dufferin, wife of Governor-General Lord Dufferin, in an 1872 entry in her book *My Canadian Journal*

✤

Quebec is the most interesting thing by much that I have seen on this Continent, and I think I would sooner be a poor priest in Quebec than a rich hog-merchant in Chicago.

British writer **Matthew Arnold** in an 1884 letter

✤

The fog lifted and everyone was pointing. A mile or so away was a gigantic fortress sailing majestically along. Pale pink in the setting sun on one side and blue-green on the other. It towered out of the water and with nine-tenths out of sight below the surface, imagination boggled at the size of the whole.

British actor **David Niven** in the 1930s, enroute to a new career in Hollywood, on first sighting the citadel at Quebec

I shall never forget my feelings on landing under the great cliff [of Quebec City] on which stands the citadel ... It seemed as though I was in France, in my dear old Brittany. It looked like St. Malo strayed up here and was lost in the snow. The illusion become complete when I saw the grey houses, heard the people talk with the Breton intonation, and saw over the shops Langlois, Maillard, Clouet, and all the names familiar to my childhood. But why say "illusion"? It was a fact: I was in France. These folks have given their faith to England; but, as the Canadian poets say, they haved kept their hearts for France. Not only their hearts, but their manners and their language. Oh, there was such pleasure in it all! The lovely weather, the beautiful scenery, the kind welcome given to me, the delight in seeing these children of old France, more than three thousand miles from home, happy and thriving— a feast for the eyes, a feast for the heart.

French travel writer **Paul Blouet** in 1891

❦

And high and grey and serene above the morning lay the citadel of Quebec. Is there any city in the world that stands so nobly as Quebec?

Rupert Brooke in 1916

❦

It is almost impossible to conceive of any urban vista more provocative of imaginative ecstasy, or the sense of magical gateways opening on an adventurous dream-world of exotic wonder, than a chance glimpse of one of these silver spires at the end of an ancient uphill or downhill street.

American author **H. P. Lovecraft** in 1931,
describing Quebec City's skyline

Quebec has marvellous restaurants, wonderful shows, and cosier cafés than those of Paris. The Quebeckers have won on their home-ground a battle lost by all other Northerners: in the teeth of the English and in spite of the snow, they have routed boredom.

French commentator **Frederic Barreyre**
in 1987

✦

There are other nuclear cities in the world into which are packed the whole record and chosen symbolism of their history: Vienna inside the Ring, Istanbul between the Blue Mosque and St. Sophia and the Topkapi. But Quebec preserves the legend and the institutions of the settlement, and its development, and its tragic fall in an almost unique intensity …

There is, to an un-French European, a comforting foreignness about old Quebec, an architecture and atmosphere that bring a sense of being away from home in the Old World, not in the infinitely more alien New World of the English-speaking states and provinces.

John Keegan, defence correspondent for
Britain's *Daily Telegraph*, in his 1995 book,
*Warpaths: Travels of a Military Historian
in North America*

✦

Montreal has something of American luxury, the sagacity of London, the briskness of New York, the gaiety of Europe.

British writer **V. S. Pritchett** in 1964

The city is the quietest and best-behaved I ever was in. We dined at the mess of the Sixtieth Rifles last night, and walked home through the heart of the city at ten-thirty. Every one had gone to bed, apparently, for there wasn't a light in fifty houses and we literally met no one—not half a dozen people certainly in the whole distance. Altogether I am very much impressed with the healthiness of the life, morally and physically, and can scarcely imagine any country I would sooner start in were I beginning life again.

English novelist and parliamentarian **Thomas Hughes**, on an 1870 visit to Montreal

❀

Montreal is pleasantly situated at the margin of the St. Lawrence, and is backed by some bold heights, about which there are charming rides and drives. The streets are generally narrow and irregular, as in most French towns of any age, but in the more modern parts of the city, they are wide and airy. They display a great variety of very good shops; and both in the town and suburbs there are many excellent private dwellings. The granite quays are remarkable for their beauty, solidity, and extent.

Charles Dickens in his 1842 memoir
American Notes

❀

You have here one of the essentials of art—sunlight. When I went up the hill beyond your lovely city I was delighted with the clear atmosphere and hope you will never let it be polluted with the smoke of factories and tall chimneys, which no man has a right to bring into your midst.

Anglo-Irish writer **Oscar Wilde** in 1882,
referring to Mount Royal Park

Put Montreal down as one of the brightest, liveliest and most charming cities—at least in winter—that can be. We got here after noon of yesterday. I can't tell you all of the pretty sights. There is much quaint of old, and not a little good new, architecture ... The dress of the Canadian people is picturesque beyond anything else in America. The furs, in endless quantity, and variety of a kind and colour, are enough to give most striking character to them ... The people have simply turned the bitter months of the year into days so full of exhilaration that there is hardly left time to sleep.

George Washington Cable, American
novelist and short-story writer, on his
impressions during an 1885 speaking
tour with Mark Twain that brought
him to Montreal

❀

It was a joy to feel the glamour of history once more as we entered Montreal. On the first day we ascended the mountain and looked down on what is one of the most wonderful views in the world—and I can speak now with some knowledge. At your feet lies the old grey town, which is spreading fast upon either flank, and which is impressive with its wealth of domes and spires ... It is no mushroom city this. It contains buildings which would be considered venerable and historical even by a European standard.

Arthur Conan Doyle in 1914

❀

Life there is vibrant, explosive and dazzling. Montreal, or the electric city.

French writer **Michel Tournier** in 1975

Montreal seems to me the highest point of hope for culture in the Western world.

German filmmaker **Rainer Werner Fassbinder** in 1981

♦

There is great cultural vitality and a *joie de vivre* unknown elsewhere in North America.

Michelin Guide to Canada on Montreal, in 1985

♦

Sometimes, in these wonderful Canadian evenings, I have looked out at that most beautiful view from my window in the Chateau Laurier and watched the afterglow over the Laurentian Hills, and the still waters of the Ottawa, and I seem to see passing along towards the hills, to the sunset, the eternal procession of mankind, emerging from the dimness and the darkness of the earliest ages, struggling, raising themselves, falling—empires and kingdoms rising and falling—and I see the procession come to my own time, when I step down and take a humble place in it, and march on with the multitude, little knowing when we came, or whether we are going.

British statesman **Stanley Baldwin** in 1927

♦

Outside, the deepening orange of the autumn sunshine was turning the copper roofs of the turreted stone government buildings to a transient shimmering gold, and I reflected, watching from the windows, that I'd much liked this graceful city when I'd been here before. I was filled with a serene sense of peace and contentment ...

British crime novelist **Dick Francis** on Ottawa in 1988

No city is more innocent of foolish pomp and feathered panoply ... The federal centre of Ottawa in all its jagged majesty seems to me still one of the most satisfying of all architectural ensembles.

Jan Morris

❦

When Queen Victoria chose Ottawa as the capital of the dominion of Canada in 1857, she had little idea of how severe the winters get. For several months a year, ice and snow virtually severed Ottawa from the rest of the country. Left to their own devices, the 10,000 Ottawans of the day learned to turn the terror of winter into joy. They gave sleigh parties, ice-skated to music, organized curling competitions and singalongs, built snowmen and ice palaces. A century later those traditions have evolved into Winterlude, North America's largest winter festival ... Even the most savage weather has been domesticated. Giant snow-removal machines clear the main arteries literally in minutes. Absent are gridlocks that mark punier snowfalls farther south ... Crammed with museums, art centres, sports arenas and good places to eat and sleep, Ottawa hangs out a big, bilingual welcome sign.

New York Times report from its
Canadian correspondent, **Clyde H. Farnsworth**,
in 1996

❦

As we approach Toronto everything looks doubly beautiful, especially the glimpses of blue Ontario's waters, sunlit, yet with slight haze, through which occasionally a distant sail ... The city made the impression on me of a lively and dashing place. The lake gives it character.

Walt Whitman on an 1880 Toronto visit

A clean-shaven, pink-faced, respectably dressed, fairly energetic, unintellectual, passably sociable, well-to-do, public-school-and-varsity sort of city.

Rupert Brooke on Toronto after a 1913 visit

✦

They certainly have attractive weather here, it's just cool enough to wear a light sweater, and terribly clear ... This is a great fruit growing country, orchards everywhere ... This place is about twice as big as Memphis. Some wonderful homes here. The streets are wide and there is no hurry. They have very English signs here—Nichols, Nichols and Nichols; Barristers, they never say lawyer. I went last night and heard Sousa's band. The streets here are full of soldiers and I am kept saluting all the time. They are very strict about this ... These Canadians are wonderful to me. So easy to get along with. They are very unselfish and good natured ... Dad would be crazy about this country, everything is so pretty now [in October], almost as colorful as our fall, and it lasts so much longer.

Billy Falkner, selections from 1918 letters to his parents posted from Toronto, where he was training to be a Royal Air Force pilot. During the half year he spent in Canada, the Oxford, Miss. native adopted the traditional Canadian spelling for his surname, and as **William Faulkner** he drew heavily on his experiences from this period in his writing

✦

I've found heaven, I live in Eden, and death's the only other step.

U.S. actor **Michael Moriarty**, who moved to Toronto in the mid-1990s

It's a nice city. It hasn't destroyed itself. It's got such enormous diversity that it's hard to describe what it lives on. Just right.

> **Jane Jacobs**, author of 1961's *The Death and Life of Great American Cities*, in 1969, reflecting on her imminent (and permanent) move to Toronto after 33 years living in New York's Greenwich Village. Jacobs is alluding to the destruction of New York landmarks such as Penn Central Station during the 1960s building boom that swept most of the continent

*

Jesse could smell the coolness of the wind that blew from the lake, and he imagined that this city was more northerly, more pure, than the cities he had known in the United States.

> **Joyce Carol Oates** on Toronto, in her 1971 novel, *Wonderland*

*

I have always had a soft spot for Canada, and particularly Toronto. People there were very kind to us at the time. When people ask me where I'd like to open a play, I always say Toronto. I've always been lucky there.

> Welsh actor **Richard Burton** in 1972. Burton starred in a Toronto production of *Hamlet* in 1964, and was married to Elizabeth Taylor in Montreal

Toronto was a unique place in those days [1940s and 1950s]. Artistic perspectives were adjusted to a strong natural state of individuality. Everybody in Canada seemed to listen to what they enjoyed, and nobody could tell them what to like, or what was popular, or what was the in thing. Even today, it is very hard to brainwash a Canadian.

U.S. jazz artist **Duke Ellington** in 1973

✦

The formerly tedious provincial capital has emerged as the world's newest great city.

Fortune magazine on Toronto, in 1974

✦

"Vandalism hits Toronto the good"—they'd found a scratch on one of the subway seat covers.

English antiquarian bookseller **Eric Korn** in 1977

✦

I've circled the planet forty-four times and I can honestly say that Toronto right now is operating better than any other city in the world. It's the most comfortable city to live in. It's the cleanest city. And it works.

Buckminster Fuller in 1978

✦

Without demeaning any of the other major centres in Canada, all of which I have played in and will continue to play in with great pleasure, Toronto has a vitality and centrality to the meaning of Canada that is possessed by no other city.

Violinist **Isaac Stern** in a 1979 Toronto speech

[It is] a marvellous cocktail between New York and London, at a human size. To me Toronto is the city in which to walk.

Umberto Eco

❧

Toronto, Canada, is the most perfect city in the Western Hemisphere.

U.S. science-fiction writer **Ray Bradbury** in 1980

❧

Our criticism went unheeded, such is the torpor with which Toronto pursues true urbanity. The fact appears to be that Toronto has very little grasp of what is required of a great city. Consider the garbage picture. It seems never to have occured to anybody in Toronto that garbage exists to be heaved into the streets. One can drive for miles without seeing so much as a banana peel in the gutter or a discarded newspaper whirling in the wind ... The subway, of which Toronto prides itself, was a laughable imitation of the real thing. The subway cars were not only spotlessly clean, but also fully illuminated. So were the stations. To New Yorkers, it was embarrassing, and we hadn't the heart to tell the subway authorities that they were light-years away from greatness.

New York Times columnist **Russell Baker** in 1980

❧

Toronto is one of the still workable cities with a future-oriented attitude.

U.S. futurist **Alvin Toffler** in 1981

If I were young and starting out I'd want to settle in either Los Angeles or Toronto. There seems to be a freedom and openness [in Toronto] I don't find elsewhere. Toronto has a real sense of opportunity and that seems to be especially true for women.

> U.S. film critic **Pauline Kael** in 1980

❀

I think it's cute.

> U.S. satirical writer **Fran Lebowitz** on Toronto,
> in 1981

❀

It's one of the most beautiful cities I've ever seen, by night and by day.

> Soviet Politburo member and future
> president **Mikhail Gorbachev** in 1983, viewing
> Toronto from atop the CN Tower

❀

Life has been very good to Toronto since I was last here. The dramatic changes in the Toronto skyline, I think, spell the message of success and prosperity … It's witness not only to the right policies but to the initiative and leadership of so many who are in this room today.

> British Prime Minister **Margaret Thatcher** in
> a 1984 Toronto speech. Her previous visit
> was in 1975

❀

New York operated by the Swiss.

> British actor and producer **Peter Ustinov**,
> on Toronto

Toronto remains a North American miracle, a city … without the decay, social squalor and unrest that characterizes so many U.S. cities, or Paris for that matter.

Editorial in *Le Nouvel Observateur*, Paris, in 1987

✦

After New York, Toronto must have the greatest contribution of restaurants of any North American city.

English travel writer **Stephen Brook** in 1987

✦

Canadians should stop being nervous and count their blessings, beginning with Toronto, which is a modern miracle—a city that has become better as it has become bigger.

U.S. political commentator **George Will** in 1988.
Will taught at the University of Toronto in the late 1960s

✦

I didn't realize how utterly pleasant it was to be here. I've come from New York, which is a warthog straight from hell.

U.S. actor **Marlon Brando** in 1989, during a Toronto film shoot

✦

A New Yorker cannot help finding Toronto a peaceful and well-kept place. That is what they find most striking. If they meant boring they would say so.

New York writer **Matt Murdoch** in 1989, puzzled on learning that Canadians often take compliments about their clean, safe country to mean that visitors find it dull

I spent the rest of the afternoon doing some shopping and walking and taxi-riding around, getting reacquainted with one of the most visually entertaining cities in the world. I'd found it architecturally exciting six years earlier, and it seemed to me now not less but more so, with glimpses of its slender tallest-in-the-world free-standing tower with the onion bulge near its top appearing tantalizingly between angular high-rises covered with black glass and gold.

> **Dick Francis** on Toronto in *The Edge*,
> in 1988

❦

Spending time recently in Toronto, at the invitation of Canada's Ukranian community, I couldn't help observing the neighbourhoods of that city—Ukranian and Jewish neighbourhoods, Polish and Chinese ones, which together made up a sort of precious alloy of differing nationalities and religions.

> Polish journalist and dissident
> **Adam Michnik** in 1990

❦

Already the most immaculate city in North America, Toronto was finally cleansed last weekend of the Jays' reputation as choke-niks.

> ***Sports Illustrated***'s report on the Blue Jays'
> triumph over the Atlanta Braves in the 1992
> World Series

Canada's hottest city is earning its place as "Silicon Valley North." A technology corridor now extends from downtown Toronto and north into the Ottawa Valley ... Toronto is expensive by North American standards. But the weak Canadian dollar makes it a better deal for foreign companies and their employees ... Many residents are willing to look beyond prices to enjoy a city that offers fine universities, a national health care system and a celebrated cultural scene.

> *Fortune*'s assessment of Toronto, selected in 1995 as one of the magazine's "Top Global Cities." The complete list, judged on market-growth potential, business infrastructure, cultural acceptance, personal risk and recruitment and entertainment: Singapore, 1; San Francisco Bay Area, 2; London, 3; New York, 4; Frankfurt, 5; Hong Kong, 6; Atlanta, 7; Toronto, 8; Paris, 9; Tokyo, 10.

✦

It was very similar to Chicago, and I mean that in a good way —not Al Capone and all that sort of stuff. It reminded me of home.

> Basketball star **Michael Jordan** of the Chicago Bulls in 1996, on why he chose Toronto for the site of his second Michael Jordan Restaurant (the first is in Chicago)

✦

New York could become something like Toronto, happy and edgeless and Canadian.

> *New York* magazine in 1996, in an article celebrating improved economic and crime conditions in the Big Apple, and heralding "the return of New York"

I love it here. It's not just the vitality of the culture, it's the pace of work—everyone's trying to get ahead, not sitting back waiting for something to happen, but always pushing themselves and their work to a higher level.

Chicago native **Patricia D. Norman**, public relations chief at the Toronto office of the United States Information Service, in 1995

❀

The Prairie is the High Veldt, plus Hope, Activity, and Reward. Winnipeg is the door to it—a great city in a great plain, comparing herself, innocently enough, to other cities of her acquaintance, but quite unlike any other city.

Rudyard Kipling in 1908

❀

When I consider the wonderful psychical phenomena of the one circle seen with my own eyes and the religious atmosphere of the other, I came away with the conclusion that Winnipeg stands very high among the places we have visited for its psychic possibilities.

Arthur Conan Doyle, lifelong spiritualist, in 1923

❀

You note the class of men going in there—that means brains; you see the endless grainlands—they mean wealth; you mark those long winter evenings—these mean time to think. There is a rare combination: brains, wealth, and time to think. I tell you there are great things coming out of the Canadian North-West. Keep your eye on Winnipeg.

Henry Ward Beecher

The citizens of Winnipeg support the company because it is fine and because the citizens are neither surfeited nor corrupted. They take joy in beautiful things.

New York choreographer **Agnes de Mille**, during a 1963 visit to the Royal Winnipeg Ballet

✦

The supply and human resource demands of World War II helped to boost Winnipeg's economy, and it has been on an upswing ever since because of the optimism, hard work and intelligence of its citizens. In the sphere of international culture, most people outside Canada may never have heard of Manitoba, but they surely know of the Royal Winnipeg Ballet, one of the foremost classical dance companies in the world. Sometimes it is difficult to reconcile in one's mind the ethos of the prairies with great cultural institutions, but in Winnipeg the blend works exceedingly well. In addition to dance, there's excellence in visual arts and in dramatic art.

U.S. travel writer **Frederick Pratson** in 1987

✦

The image of the Old West persists in Calgary—it annually holds the largest rodeo in the world, the Calgary Stampede, and authentic cattle ranches with real cowhands are but a short drive from city limits—yet Calgary can be best equated with such great cities of Texas as Dallas and Fort Worth ... The prosperity brought by the petroleum industry is reflected in the affluence of most of the people who live here, the modern city itself, and the recreational and cultural amenities it offers to residents and visitors ... [It is] a former Northwest Mounted Police post that in less than a hundred years has become a booming, gleaming, twenty-first-century city, very much in a class by itself.

Frederick Pratson in 1987

Although the dominent ethnic group is British, Regina is a cosmopolitan city in which many different cultures merge and contribute their own unique flavours and perspectives. The bottom line here, regardless of one's heritage, is good old-fashioned prairie friendliness.

Frederick Pratson in 1987

❋

With my wife and son I had left England for Canada only a few months before and we were none of us yet accustomed to the great steely neonlit city which lay on the foothills of the Rockies more than three thousand feet up. The sky seemed higher and larger than our English skies, above the level of the clouds we knew, and the air was cold and fresh like lake water. From our bungalow which was called Kosy Nuick on the outskirts of the city we could see across the rolling beige ranchland to the snowy peaks of the Rockies; they changed colour every hour of the day—sometimes they were a hard glittering white, sometimes a pale rose and even at moments a deep blue like storm clouds. I only mention these effects to show that we did not feel in the least exiled in the far West. If anything there was a sense of exhilaration, of freedom, and of a new life beginning.

British novelist **Graham Greene** in a short story, "Dear Dr. Falkenheim," that is set in Calgary. Greene spent three Christmases with his daughter, Caroline, at her Alberta ranch, where he wrote a large portion of *Our Man in Havana*

Dark worries attend every modern Olympiad. Besides a delicious forum for political commentary, the Games present an international spotlight for terrorists. But in the bright face of this city, treachery has become a distant concern, as Organizing Committee Chairman Frank King has indicated in his wonderful proclamation, "The prospects of problems that are large are small." Asked about the unfailing good humour of every bus driver and security guard in Western Canada, King cited the region's natural resistance to cynicism, "almost a central naivete."

> *Time* writer **Tom Callahan** on the 1988 Winter Olympics in Calgary, which won international acclaim for the spirit of volunteerism among Calgarians and the effort to prevent the widespread price gouging among local merchants and restaurateurs that marked the previous Winter Games in Lake Placid, N.Y.

❖

To lovers of malls and theme parks, the West Edmonton Mall and Galaxy Land makes Edmonton special. To business wheeler-dealers working the rich oil and natural gas fields near the city, Edmonton is prime playing field. To those who want the magnificence of the great national parks of the Canadian Rockies with their resorts and many recreational opportunities, Edmonton's proximity to Jasper and Banff makes it special. And to those who want to kick up their heels at a rip-roaring festival, the rooting-tooting Klondike Days do ... Edmonton is a city of grace, vitality, culture and vision.

Frederick Pratson in 1987

Cities in North America don't come any more glittering than Calgary, a likeable place whose impressive downtown sky-scrapers rose almost overnight on the back of an oil boom in the Seventies to turn it into Canada's very own Dallas. The tight high-rise core is good for wandering, and contains Calgary's most prestigious sight, the Glenbow Museum, while the simple wooden houses of the far-flung suburbs show a different, homelier side to the city, recalling its pioneering frontier origins.

Tim Jepson, Phil Lee and **Tania Smith**
in 1992

❋

Hardly any area of entertainment goes uncelebrated by a festival at some time of the year in Edmonton ... The Edmonton Folk Music Festival, rated the best in North America by Rolling Stone, [is] held at Gallagher Park at the end of the first week in August. Also well regarded are the International Street Performers Festival in early July; the International Jazz City Festival at the end of June; and the August Fringe Festival, a nine-day theatrical jamboree that's the largest event of its kind in North America.

Tim Jepson, Phil Lee and **Tania Smith**
in 1992

❋

A great sleepiness lies on Vancouver as compared with the American town; men don't fly up and down the streets telling lies, and the spitoons in the delightfully comfortable hotel are unused; the baths are free and the doors are unlocked ... An American bade me notice the absence of bustle, and was alarmed when in a loud and audible voice I thanked God for it.

Rudyard Kipling in 1889, during the first of at
least seven visits to Canada

It's a great place, rather different from the rest of Canada. More oriental. The country and harbour are rather beautiful with great violet mountains all round, snow-peaks in the distance.

Rupert Brooke in a 1913 letter to his mother, posted from Vancouver

❦

Vancouver is lovely. There is no other word for it. High, snow-capped mountains dominate the town, and the land-locked, green-shored bay with its pellucid waters makes a wonderful setting. The town, itself, is very American in appearance with its high buildings. Here also there can be no great expansion until Western Canada is more populous, but sooner or later Vancouver will certainly be another San Francisco.

Arthur Conan Doyle in 1923

❦

So far we have not budged a step, and shall not unless Hitler pushes us out by the scruffs of our necks. In that case we shall certainly come to Canada, as we have a joint annuity there to die on. And Vancouver is the pick of Canada.

George Bernard Shaw in 1940, musing on relocation prospects during the Battle of Britain

❦

Captain Vancouver could hardly have foreseen today's great, clanging port of roughly a million people, third-largest city in Canada. It has become an outdoorsman's paradise where 40,000 pleasure craft nestle in a labyrinthine harbour with a shoreline a hundred miles long.

U.S. writer and editor **Berry Reece** in 1967

I had fallen in love with Vancouver instantly, this city where it rains all day long and then produces the most sublime sunsets. It's impossible to paint here! The intoxication of impotence! The canvas stays blank while you feast your eyes! It was a drug and I wanted to test its powers to the full before moving on.

Michel Tournier in his 1975 novel, *Gemeni*

❀

Vancouver enjoys one of the most splendid of all city settings —better than San Francisco's because of the greenness, better than Sydney's, because of the mountains all around, rivalled perhaps only by Rio and Hong Kong.

Jan Morris

❀

Vancouver is an important place to be, maybe even more important than Ottawa. The city is overflowing with information about Asia-Pacific countries, with interesting thinkers in science and technology and with lots of experimentation. It's an important port.

Conrado Beckerman, Consul General at Uruguay's Vancouver consulate, in 1995, explaining why more than a dozen countries have either opened new consulates in Vancouver or upgraded their offices to full-time operations since 1990

At one time you had Montreal on the St. Lawrence, then Toronto on the Great Lakes. Now there's a new place booming, thriving with the economy of the future, based on high-tech and open to the Pacific Rim. We want to be part of that, from here, from Vancouver.

> **Alfred Siefer-Gaillardin**, French ambassador to
> Canada, in 1995, on France's increased diplo-
> matic presence in Vancouver. "It's true we
> feel at home in Quebec, but Canada cannot
> be reduced to Quebec," said Siefer-Gaillardin,
> explaining that French diplomats need to
> have "personal contact with this new reality
> of Canada."

❧

The place itself appears a perfect Eden in the midst of the dreary wilderness of the Northwest coast, and so different in its general aspect … that one might be pardoned for supposing it had dropped from the clouds.

> **James Douglas, Jr.** in 1842, on Victoria

❧

The retired wheat-grower or miner in the evening of his days could find no more pleasant waiting place.

> **Arthur Conan Doyle** in 1923, on Victoria

❧

Dear Mama: This is a beautiful little city, and the capital of British Columbia—Like its name it is Victorian and seems very slow and quaint after the U.S.

> American novelist **Thomas Wolfe**, in a
> 1938 postcard to his mother,
> Mrs. Julia Elizabeth Wolfe

To realize Victoria you must take all that the eye admires most in Bournemouth, Torquay, the Isle of Wight, the Happy Valley at Hong Kong, the Doon, Sorrento, and Camps Bay; add reminiscences of the Thousand Islands, and arrange the whole round the Bay of Naples, with some Himalayas for the background. Real estate agents recommend it as a little piece of England—the island on which it stands is about the size of Great Britain—but no England is set in any such seas or so fully charged with the mystery of the larger ocean beyond. The high, still twilights along the beaches are out of the old East just under the curve of the world, and even in October the sun rises warm from the first. Earth, sky, and water wait outside every man's door to drag him out to play if he looks up from his work; and, though some other cities in the Dominion do not quite understand this immoral mood of Nature, men who have made their money in them go off to Victoria, and with the zeal of converts preach and preserve its beauties.

Rudyard Kipling in 1908

❦

Some players don't like it in Montreal. You know why? They don't give it a chance. But I learned there to take an interest in the French culture, learn some French and respond to the community. The people were very appreciative. (My wife) Michele and I really connected with the city. We had a lot of fun there.

> New York Yankees pitcher **John Wetteland**, a native of California, in 1996, on his desire to be traded back to the Montreal Expos, where he was a star between 1992 and 1994 until he was sent to New York as part of a salary purge. "I'd play for peanuts in Montreal," said Wetteland, "I loved it there."

CULTURE & ENTERPRISE

The fisheries of Newfoundland are inexhaustible and are of more value to the Empire than all the silver mines of Peru ... greater than the gold mines of Golgonda, there is none so rich.

English essayist **Francis Bacon** in 1608

❖

I am having charming audiences, you will be glad to hear; the Canadians are very appreciative people, but it is a great fight in this commercial age to plead the cause of Art. Still the principles which I represent are so broad, so grand, so noble, that I have no fear for the future.

Irish author **Oscar Wilde** in an 1882 letter
written from Halifax

❖

You fellows in Canada are doing the best work that is being done by your contemporaries in the English language.

British poet **Algernon Charles Swinburne** in
1899, remark to Canadian poet
Charles G.D. Roberts

I was agreeably surprised when I came here to see what a fine country it was. It being excellent land, bearing crops of wheat and other corn for twenty or thirty years without any dung. Here you have no rent to pay, no poor-rates, and scarcely any taxes. No game-keepers or lords over you. Here you can go and shoot wild deer, Turkeys, Pheasants, Quails, Pigeons, any other sort of game and catch plenty of fish without molestation whatever; here you can raise everything of your own that you want to make use of in your family. You can make your own soap, candles, sugar, treacle and vinegar without paying any duty. Clothing is as cheap as in England. Wages is high … a man can earn enough in three days to last him all the week. I am satisfied with the country and so is Luesa, for we are so much respected here as any of our neighbours, and so would you if you come.

> **Philip Annett**, day-labourer and emigrant to
> Upper Canada, in an 1830 letter

*

You talk with him and it is as if Canada stands before you, telling her astonishing story.

> **A. G. Gardiner**, editor of the *London Daily
> News*, on an encounter with the Illinois-born
> William Cornelius van Horne, driving force
> behind the construction of the Canadian
> Pacific Railway and a fierce Canadian
> nationalist. Horne himself said: "To have
> built that road would have made a
> Canadian out of the German Emperor."

Thus, what is in progress in Canada during the opening years of the twentieth century is not the normal growth of a settled community, but the rapid—almost the sudden—economic appropriation of a new land. To the economist, the discovery of Canada will date, not from Jacques Cartier or its acquisition from Wolfe, but from the opening of the "C.P.R." (Canadian Pacific Railway) in 1886. The present inhabitants of Canada are a race of conquerors.

Beatrice and Sidney Webb, British socialists who
visited Canada in 1911 to supply a report to
the Poor-Law Commission

✦

I feel, gentlemen, here in Canada that I am standing at a place which must in the process of time produce a very great literature. When I put it in the future I do not mean that it has not yet done so, but what I mean is that it will be a great volume of literature which in time to come may well influence the literature of the world.

Arthur Conan Doyle in a 1914 Montreal speech on
the future of Canadian literature

✦

I think the fact that the telephone was invented in Canada should be more widely known than it is—at least in the United States ... We did not hear very much about the "Red Wing" [an early aircraft that was aloft in 1908 in New York] in the United States, because the aviator was Canadian, Mr. Baldwin. He was the first man to get into air in public in America.

Alexander Graham Bell in a 1917 Empire Club of
Canada speech. Bell was referring to Toronto
aviator F.W. (Casey) Baldwin

When Lord Selkirk set out, a friend who heard of his project said to him, "Sir, if you are bent on doing something futile, why do you not sow tares at home in order to reap wheat, or plough the desert of Sahara, which is so much nearer?" Today we can smile at that in knowledge that the greatest wheat market of the world is almost on the site of Lord Selkirk's settlement.

Stanley Baldwin in 1927, referring to Manitoba's
Red River Colony, established
in present-day Winnipeg in 1812

✦

I would like to take this opportunity to emphasize that the credit of the first definite proof of atomic transformation belongs to McGill University. It was in the Macdonald Building in the years 1902–04 that Soddy and I accumulated the experimental evidence that the radioactive elements were undergoing spontaenous transformation.

Nobel laureate scientist **Ernest Rutherford**,
one-time McGill researcher, in 1932; the
reference is to his assistant, Frederick Soddy

✦

Point the way to a wiser use of this scientific boon that we have let fall into unworthy keeping … We look to you in Canada to lead radio in North America out of the morass in which it is pitiably sunk. May Canada fulfill my early dream!

American scientist **Lee de Forest** in 1932,
urging the creation of what would become
the Canadian Broadcasting Corp.

The drama is in a happy position in Canada. It has such strong supporters!

> British director **Harley Granville-Barker**
> in 1936

♣

When I learned that provincial Canada had drawn easily ahead of Pasteurized Pavloffed Freudized Europe, and made professors of men who were in the vanguard instead of among the stragglers and camp followers, I found myself considering seriously, especially when the German airman dropped a bomb near enough to shake my house, whether I had not better end my days in Vancouver, if not in Saskatoon.

> **George Bernard Shaw** in 1948

♣

In the days to come I believe you will produce a native poet who will break away from the past as sharply as Walt Whitman did; a poet who will never be mistaken for anything but a Canadian, and who will find in the challenging space of your prairies and forests his greatest themes.

> *Atlantic Monthly* editor **Edward Weeks**
> in a 1955 Toronto speech

♣

A thousand years from now people will know Montreal as the place where Wilder Penfield made his classic maps of the cerebral cortex, Hans Seyle made "stress" a household word, and Jacques Genest helped to blaze a trail through the Laurentian mountains to an understanding of hypertension.

> **R. S. Morison**, director of Medical and Natural
> Sciences, Rockefeller Foundation, in 1964

Confronted with, involved with Canada, the coy colossus, poets will have to be ambitious and bold.

> British writer **Paul West**, once an
> instructor at Newfoundland's Memorial
> University, in 1960

❦

Canada has never had a major war. After hockey, Canadians would probably have found it dull.

> **Jim Brosnan**, former American major-league
> baseball pitcher

❦

It is no exaggeration to say that not a single Soviet library, either town or village library, is without books by such popular writers as Ernest Seton-Thompson [sic], Stephen Leacock, Charles George Roberts, etc.

> Russian commentator **V. Makhotin** in 1974

❦

Oh, how I respect the courage with which the English and French have collaborated to turn that arduous realm into a vivacious and creative environment.

> U.S. popular philosopher **Will Durant**, author of
> *The Story of Philosophy*, on Canada in 1979

❦

Canada does have a neo-Canadian look: subdued, restrained, in good taste, not at all American.

> U.S. novelist **Mary McCarthy** in 1982,
> on Canadian apparel fashions

I like Canada and your people because you are so practical. You dress for warmth and for function, and function of course is the basis of all good design.

French couturier **André Courrèges** in 1983

❦

For years I've been on the Academy Awards' documentary selection committee and the work we see from Canada has a flair for ideas which is unique.

Ray Bradbury in 1987

❦

If you're a writer, it's attractive to find new territory … I've heard Canadian writers talk about the way in which Canadian literature is gradually building an imaginative map of the country. I think it's rather wonderful for the writer to be in a place where there is still a lot to be done. In England, you can't take a step without falling over somebody else's book, or somebody else's patch of ground. Every piece of London has blue plaques on it where writers used to live and which they have written about, so to be able to find a metropolis that had not been written about was a gift. It attracted me for reasons that have nothing to do with politics or race, to say look at this, it's an interesting rich world and it's right next door.

Anglo-Indian novelist **Salman Rushdie** in 1989, interviewed at Harbourfront's International Festival of Authors in Toronto

One thing I always like about playing Toronto—they never booed.

> **Sparky Anderson** in 1983. Anderson, the only
> man to manage World Series champions in
> both the National and American leagues (the
> 1975 and 1976 Cincinnati Reds and the 1984
> Detroit Tigers), made his managerial debut
> with the Toronto Maple Leafs of the
> International League, for whom he
> also played second base—by all
> accounts rather poorly

❦

I have a sort of romantic sentiment about it. I think that Canada in a literary sense is a very Nordic country. It has its long winters and it has its Nordic glooms as well as its other passions. It has a very high readership ratio to the population by comparison with other nations. And publishing has just taken off here ... I had that sense of, maybe it's terribly dangerous to say it, of lost Europeans which I also had in the Soviet Union; of people with a tremendous cultural appetite and with a great intellectual reach.

John le Carré in 1989

❦

It's astonishing how many countries now produce good wine. The Indians make a decent champagne. Lebanese wine is superb. Chilean isn't bad. There's some nice Canadian wine, believe it or not, though I recommend you avoid at all costs something called "Cold Duck."

Simon Hoggart in London's *Observer Magazine* in 1990

Despite continued American sniping and a financial situation of continuing precariousness the Canadians showed the world that they could build a transcontinental railway honestly and quickly ... [Like the U.S., Canada] also had a long tradition of using "Dominion" (public) lands to encourage settlement and development. But whereas the Americans favoured checkerboard grants, the Canadian grants consisted of unified chunks, designed to provide compact groups of homesteads. As a result, the Canadian Pacific was endowed with 25 million acres of Dominion lands, far and away the biggest grant to any single railway in the world. This vast area, as big as England, was integrated with the homesteads occupied by individual settlers far more harmoniously than in the United States. A tenth of this land had been improved thanks to the biggest single irrigation project ever undertaken by a railway, or anyone else in the world, up to that point.

In all, the CPR fostered some 800 towns and cities in the three prairie provinces.

> British author **Nicholas Faith** in *The World The Railways Made* (1990), on the economic impact of Canada's first transcontinental railway, the Canadian Pacific

◆

On a per capita basis Canadians own far more of the United States than vice versa.

> **Seymour Lipset**, Stanford University professor and author of *Continental Divide: The Institutions and Values of The United States and Canada*, in 1990. Lipset was quoted by Andrew H. Malcolm in a *New York Times* report noting that many Canadians "have come to resent the widespread presence" of U.S. firms in their economic

life, "but in recent years the corporate shoe has been moving to the other foot ... The United States had long been the largest foreign investor in Canada, with about $62 billion of direct investment there in 1988 ... But now, according to the Canadian Government, Canada has $34.5 billion of direct investments in the United States, up from $30.3 billion in 1987."

✦

Canada has produced some of America's funniest comedians, actors, writers, directors a veritable army of renegade humour professionals. Without them, there would have been no *Saturday Night Live*, no *SCTV*, no *Spy* magazine, no *Ghostbusters*, no *Wayne's World*, no sidekick for David Letterman to take with him to CBS. Expatriate Canucks like Dan Ackroyd, Michael J. Fox, Mike Myers, Phil Hartman, John Candy, Rick Moranis and Martin Short could gather on Thursday to celebrate Canada Day ...

Thanks to their near indetectable accent and their proximity to the United States, Canadians have insinuated themselves into the pop culture of the United States, from Mary Pickford ("America's Sweetheart") to the Amazing Kreskin. *Field of Dreams*, the mythic movie about the great American pastime, was based on the baseball novel *Shoeless Joe*, by the Canadian W.P. Kinsella. Television is filled with Canadians, from Lorne Greene in reruns of *Bonanza* and the space cowboy William Shatner on *Star Trek* to Jason Priestley, the hearthrob on *Beverly Hills 90210*. *Generation X*, the bible of the 20-somethings, was written by a Canadian. Even Superman, defender of truth, justice and the American way, was the invention of Joe Shuster, from Toronto.

Rick Marin, "The Most Entertaining Americans? Canadians," *New York Times* report in 1993

At the Toronto film festival you're greeted by a warm welcome and a cold beer, which is the exact opposite of Cannes.
British journalist **Iain Johnstone** in 1990

❖

Authors from Britain's former colonies have begun to capture
the very heart of English literature, transforming the canon
with bright colours and strange cadences and foreign eyes.
They are revolutionizing the language from within. Hot spices
are entering English, and tropical birds and sorcerers—magical creations from the makers of a new World Ficton.

All are writers not of Anglo-Saxon ancestry, born more or
less after the war, and choosing to write in English. All are
situated at a crossroads from which they can reflect, and
reflect on, our increasingly small, increasingly mongrel,
increasingly mobile global village. The centres of this new
frontierless kind of writing are the growing capitals of multicultural life, such as London, Toronto and, to a lesser extent,
New York, but the form is rising up wherever cultures jangle ...

A typical capital of this blossoming multicultural order is
Toronto, which [editor Sonny Mehta at New York publishing
house Alfred A. Knopf] calls "the new literary centre of the
northern hemisphere." [Michael] Ondaatje has brought out
an anthology of Canadian writing that includes the voices of
immigrants from Malta, South Africa and the Caribbean, and
in the literary magazine he co-edits in Toronto he can call upon
such distinguished local exiles as the Pole Josef Skvorecky
and the Indian Rohinton Mistry. The city draws further energy from such traditional masters as Margaret Atwood and
Robertson Davies. The Canadian government has done
much to sponsor readings and writings. At the city's annual
International Festival of Authors at Harbourfront, scores of
international writers regularly address audiences of 500.

Anglo-American novelist **Pico Iyer** in a 1993
Time cover story on a new literary school of
"global" writers that began with Salman
Rushdie and Kazuo Ishiguro, and includes
1992 Booker Prize co-winner Michael
Ondaatje (for *The English Patient*), "a Sri
Lankan of Indian, Dutch and English ances-
try, educated in Britain, long resident in
Canada, with siblings on four continents."

❦

Being in existence for a mere 17 years hasn't allowed time
for the Jays to create storied rivalries, such as Yankees-Red
Sox or Dodgers-Giants; those teams have been going at each
other since the turn of the century. But winning has a way of
accelerating the process. Considering the Jays have nestled
atop the American League East division seemingly every year
for the last decade, it's only natural for resentment to grow
among division foes. Each has a tale to tell ...

A 1955 Broadway play had Washington Senators player
Joe Hardy selling his soul to the devil in a deal to beat the
Damn Yankees. Judging by the frustration of most AL East
fans and their teams, it's time for a sequel. Certainly the
thought has crossed their minds during the past several years,
watching the Blue Jays go after title after title. Go ahead, don't
deny the feeling any longer. Say it. Say it! *Damn Blue Jays*.

USA Today Baseball Weekly in 1993, as the Jays
were putting the finishing touches on their
eleventh consecutive winning season, and
preparing for their second straight
World Series championship

It is without cause that some Canadians tend to be sheepish about their native food and wines. The sense of being in the shadow of their neighbour to the south has made many Canadian food professionals into seekers after some homogenized "international cuisine." Happily the chef at Rundles [a Stratford, Ont. restaurant] is not among them; instead he shows a passion for fresh Canadian ingredients. In the off season the restaurant collaborates with other Stratford-area restaurants to operate a demanding and acclaimed chefs' school. Here the best of local field and stream is unabashedly matched with some fine Canadian wines from places such as the Niagara peninsula and Pelee Island.

> U.S. broadcaster **Gene Burns** in a 1994
> travel story on Stratford, Ont. in
> *The Atlantic Monthly*

❧

We are deeply indebted to your culture. Our daughter's name was inspired by Canadian songwriter Joni Mitchell's wonderful song, "Chelsea Morning" ... Our horizons have broadened because we have listened in the United States to the CBC. And our culture is much richer because of the contributions of writers like Robertson Davies, whom Hillary had the pleasure of meeting last week after reading him for years, and Margaret Atwood and because of the wonderful photography of Yousuf Karsh, whose famous picture of Churchill I just saw ... And as a musician, I have to thank you especially for Oscar Peterson, a man I consider to be the greatest jazz pianist of our time.

> President **Bill Clinton** in a 1995 House of
> Commons address

Funny you should mention Canada. The country has its share of expert film comedians, but Jim Carrey takes the cake. And the icing too. The day before the opening of *Batman Forever* —he plays the Riddler—the rubber-faced Carrey, 33, signed with Columbia to make a single film for a record $20 million. Smokin'!

> *Time* selects Jim Carrey, a product of
> Toronto's stand-up comedy scene, as one
> of "the best people of 1995"

❖

For all the concern about their survival, Canadian cultural industries have integrated themselves profitably into the North American, and global, canvas. In little more than a decade, Toronto has become the No. 3 film and television production centre in North America, behind New York City and Los Angeles. The Toronto Film Festival is considered the best industry draw on the continent. Hundreds of production companies have sprung up in Toronto, led by Alliance Communications, which sold the prime-time TV series *Due South* to CBS. Vancouver is North America's No. 4 production site, and Montreal is coming on strong.

> Excerpt from "A Nation Blessed, A Nation
> Stressed," a 1995 *Time* cover story on Canada

Toronto's annual film festival has muscled its way past competitors to become the fourth most important in the world, according to *Weekly Variety*. In a recently published poll of 100 international film executives, Cannes came in first, Berlin next, then Venice and Toronto, making this event ... the most prominent on the continent.

"We consider Toronto the premier North American festival," said Harvey Weinstein, the co-chairman of Miramax, which sent eleven staff members and eleven films to the festival. "The press is there. It's a wonderful opportunity to launch movies. There are presentations, in movie theatres, with audiences who love movies."

Joe Roth, the chairman of the live-action film division of Walt Disney Studios, which used the festival to introduce *Unstrung Heroes* in North America, said, "For the domestic [U.S.] market, Toronto is the most important festival there is."

With roughly three hundred films being screened at Toronto, it is often hard for the 1,200 movie buyers and sellers, the six hundred journalists and the passionate local movie fans to find the gold. By a rough calculation, 38 films from the 1994 festival opened to acclaim in the United States.

New York Times report on the Toronto
International Film Festival in 1995

❧

There are a number of very creative people who don't want to leave Canada, so we are coming to them.

Tom Ruzicat, senior vice-president, Walt Disney
Television Animation, in 1995, on Walt Disney
Co.'s decision to open animation
studios in Toronto and Vancouver

The same amount of research and development you can buy in the United States for one dollar costs just 52 cents in Canada ... Engineering talent costs approximately 35 per cent less in Canada than in the United States. The cost advantages of engineering in Canada, coupled with the excellence of the education system and the richness of government support for research, tell a powerful and convincing story of those key competitive advantages that Canada can offer any multinational that is contemplating investing in Canada.

> Chicago native **Daniel J. Branda**, president and
> CEO of Hewlett-Packard (Canada) Ltd., in
> 1995. HP Canada is a subsidiary of Hewlett-
> Packard Co. of Palo Alto, Calif.

MODEL NATION AND WORLD CITIZEN

It was the 28th of October 1830, in the morning when my feet first touched the Canada shore. I threw myself on the ground, rolled in the sand, seized handfulls of it and kissed them, and danced around till, in the eyes of several who were present, I passed for a madman.

> Rev. **Josiah Henson**, the liberated slave whose life, more than any other, was the basis for novelist Harriet Beecher Stowe's character Uncle Tom. The real-life Henson started a thriving collective farm near Dresden, Ont., with other refugees who had arrived on the underground railroad

❖

I was born in Maysville, Ky. I got here last Tuesday evening, and spent the Fourth of July in Canada. I felt as big and free as any man could feel, and I worked part of the day for my own benefit: I guess my master's time is out. Seventeen came away in the same gang that I did.

> U.S. fugitive slave **Ben Blackburn**, who settled in Windsor, Ont.

I had rather live in Canada, on one potato a day, than to live in the South with all the wealth they have got.

Mrs. Christopher Hamilton, a Mississippi slave, who settled in London, Ont.

❖

The policy which the United States actually pursues is the infatuated one of rejecting and spurning vigorous and ever-growing Canada, while seeking to establish feeble states out of decaying Spanish provinces on the coast and islands of the Gulf of Mexico. I shall not live to see it, but the man is already born who will see the United States mourn over this stupendous folly.

Future U.S. secretary of state **William H. Seward**, one of the most ardent in a long line of pro-annexationists, in 1857

❖

I see in British North America a region grand enough for the seat of a great empire. I find its inhabitants vigourous, hardy, energetic ... I find them jealous of the United States and of Great Britain, as they ought to be; and therefore, when I look at their extent and resources, I know that they can neither be conquered by the former nor permanently held by the latter. They will be independent, as they are already self-maintaining.

William H. Seward in 1857

Don't you think England (if we petition her humbly enough) might be induced to receive the New England States back again, in our old Provincial capacity? What a triumph that would be! Or perhaps it would be a better scheme to arrange a kingdom for Prince Alfred by lumping together Canada, New England, and Nova Scotia. Those regions are almost homogenous as regards manners and character and cannot long be kept apart, after we lose the counterbalance of our Southern States. For my part, I should be very glad to exchange the South for Canada.

> American novelist **Nathaniel Hawthorne**, in an
> 1860 letter to a friend in England, on the eve
> of the U.S. Civil War

✦

Here at last is a state whose life is not narrowly concentrated in a despot or a class, but feels itself in every limb; a government which is not a mere application of force from without, but dwells as a vital principle in the will of every citizen.

> American poet, critic and scholar **James Russell
> Lowell** in 1865, on Canada

✦

The experiment of confederation has now succeeded, and, at one bound, Canada has become a great power, from whatever point of view you like to look ... If we prefer the test of general prosperity as evidenced by the wealth of the country, an even more startling state of things meets us. There are more people in the Dominion in proportion to population than any other country in the world who are worth $1000. Such results speak for themselves as to the character of the people, who are as enterprizing and thrifty as any branch of the English-speaking race. They are already far more numerous, and more united than the thirteen colonies were at the declaration of Independence ninety-five years ago.

English novelist and parliamentarian
Thomas Hughes in 1871

✦

Its School System, founded on the Massachusetts plan, is one of the best and most comprehensive in the world.

Some of the good people of Ontario have complained in my hearing of faults and fraudulencies, commissive and omissive, on the part of their government, but I guess said people have reason to bless their stars at the general fairness, economy, wisdom and liberality of their officers and administration.

Walt Whitman in 1880

✦

I suppose no patriotic American can look at all these things, however idly, without reflecting on the ultimate possibility of their becoming absorbed into his own huge state…What the change may bring of comfort or of grief to the Canadians themselves, will be for them to say; but, in the breast of this sentimental tourist of ours, it will produce little but regret. The foreign elements of eastern Canada, at least, are extremely interesting; and it is of good profit to us Americans to have near us, and of easy access, an ample something which is not our expansive selves. Here we find a hundred mementoes of an older civilization than our own, of different manners, of social forces once mighty and glowing with a sort of autumnal warmth.

Henry James in an 1883 travelogue, based on
1871 travels in Canada

May peace and prosperity be forever the blessing of Canada, for she has been the asylum to my friends, and she is now an asylum to myself.

Jefferson Davis in an 1867 reception at Niagara Falls, Ont. Ultimately amnestied, Davis and his family lived in exile in Montreal while the U.S. Confederacy leader awaited trial for treason

❖

The local and provincial governments are the same in the Canadian towns and provinces as they are in the American towns and States: a house of representatives, a senate, and a governor. With this difference, this great difference, to the present advantage of Canada: whereas every four years the Americans elect a new master, who appoints a ministry responsible to him alone, the Canadians have a ministry responsible to their Parliament—that is, to themselves. The representation of the American people at Washington is democratic, but the Government is autocratic. In Canada, both legislature and executive are democratic, as in England, that greatest and truest of all democracies.

Paul Blouet in his 1891 travel memoir, *A Frenchman in America*

❖

Always the marvel—to which Canadians seem insensible— was that on one side of an imaginary line should be Safety, Law, Honour, and Obedience, and on the other, frank, brutal decivilization; and that despite this, Canada should be impressed by any aspect whatever of the United States.

Rudyard Kipling, during a 1907 speaking tour in Canada

My race remembers with most tender gratitude the generosity and kindness manifested on the part of the people of the Dominion of Canada in the dark days of slavery. I remember as a child hearing my parents and the older slaves speak of Canada with such tenderness and faith for what it would do for our race that I had no definite idea that it had any tangible, visible place. I thought it was an invisible ideal.

Civil rights advocate **Booker T. Washington** in a 1906 Ottawa speech

✿

You have a splendid example of the legitimate, the indispensible, the eminently useful police force in Canada—the Northwest Mounted Police.

Charles W. Eliot, president of Harvard University, in a 1907 Ottawa speech

✿

We in England have got too much into the habit of regarding the Government to some extent as our enemy ... The Government of Canada seems to me like a wise old gardener going around with its watering-pot, which contains the most precious water of Capital, and using it just where it will do most good, from one side of your great country to another.

Arthur Conan Doyle in a 1914 Ottawa address

✿

It is our intention to follow in the footsteps of Canada.

Louis Botha, Boer War general and South African statesman, referring in a 1927 speech to how the legislation creating the Union of South Africa in 1909 was modelled in part on the British North America Act of 1867

Do not encourage any enterprise looking into Canada's annexation of the United States. You are one of the most capable governing peoples of the world, but I entreat you, for your own sakes, to think twice before undertaking management of the territory which lies between the Great Lakes and the Rio Grande.

> U.S. President **Warren G. Harding** in a 1923
> Vancouver speech. The post-First World War
> era marked the final break with pro-annexa-
> tionist sentiments that had found voice in
> Washington, D.C. since before the
> Revolutionary War

❦

Someday someone will live here and be able to appreciate the feeling with which I launched *Ulysses* on the States (not a copy lost) from this city.

> **Ernest Hemingway**, *Toronto Star* reporter and
> future novelist, in a letter to Ezra Pound. In
> 1923, Hemingway smuggled into the U.S. the
> first copies of James Joyce's novel, which had
> been banned in the U.S. but not Canada

❦

Canada … is a magnet exercising a double attraction drawing both Great Britain and the United States towards herself and thus drawing them closer to each other. She is the only surviving bond which stretches from Europe across the Atlantic Ocean. In fact, no state, no country, no band of men can more truly be described as the linchpin of peace and world progress.

> **Winston Churchill** in a 1930 *Saturday*
> *Evening Post* article

There is true liberty up North. Nobody is limited in his free-dom, the banner of the sons of the Golden North is the ban-ner of the freest men on earth. Whatever you see you can go after, everything is yours, there is nothing to stop you.

Czech traveller **Jan Weizel** in 1932

❋

Here at the gateway of Canada, in mighty lands which have never known the totalitarian tyrannies of Hitler and Mussolini, the spirit of freedom has found a safe and abiding home. Here that spirit is no wandering phantom.

Winston Churchill in a 1943 London,
England speech

❋

Canada is a nation founded on a union of two great races. The harmony of their partnership is an example to all mankind —an example everywhere in the world.

U.S. President **Franklin Roosevelt** in a 1943
House of Commons address

❋

Canada emphasizes the professionalism of politics by mak-ing the leader of the Opposition a paid officer of the state.

U.S. Supreme Court justice **Felix Frankfurter**
in 1945

❋

Canada is clean, healthy, young, polite, unspoiled and, as I say, just upstairs.

New York travel writer **Horace Sutton** in 1950

The composition of your population and the evolution of your political institutions hold a lesson for the other nations of the earth. Canada has achieved internal unity and material strength, and has grown in stature in the world community, by solving problems that might have hopelessly divided and weakened a less gifted people ... Canada's eminent position today is a tribute to the patience, tolerance, and strength of character of her people of both French and British strains. For Canada is enriched by the heritage of France as well as of Britain, and Quebec has imparted the vitality and spirit of France itself to Canada. Canada's notable achievement of national unity and progress through accommodation, moderation and forbearance can be studied with profit by her sister nations.

U.S. President **Harry Truman** in a 1947 House of
Commons address

◆

Canada proved herself there [on the Western Front], and it could never be the same Canada again, as her subsequent history has already shown. Vimy Ridge was followed by Passchendaele and Amiens, to mention only the highlights. Canada had found her secure place in the great world. There her title-deeds to the future were written.

Jan Christian Smuts, prime minister of the
Union of South Africa, in 1950

◆

Canada has no cultural unity, no linguistic unity, no religious unity, no economic unity, no geographic unity. All it has is unity.

University of Michigan economics professor
Kenneth Boulding in 1957

In that conflict [World War II], and then through the more
recent and savage and grievous Korean battles, the Canadian
people have been valorous champions of freedom for mankind. Within the framework of NATO, in the construction of
new patterns for international security, in the lengthy and
often toilsome exploration of a regional alliance, they have
been patient and wise devisers of a stout defence for the
Western world ... Canada, rich in natural gifts, far richer in
human character and genius, has earned the gratitude and
the affectionate respect of all who cherish freedom and seek
peace.

U.S. President Dwight D. Eisenhower in a 1953
House of Commons address

❀

The United Nations has come to expect in its debates to hear
from Canada the voice of reason and enlightenment, rejecting
the extreme of partisanship, seeking patiently the common
ground for men of good will, yet always standing firm upon
the basic principles and purposes of our world organization.

Dag Hammarskjold, U.N. Secretary-General, in a
1954 Toronto address

❀

The Canadian spirit is cautious, observant and critical where
the American is assertive; the foreign policies of the two
nations are never likely to fit very conveniently, and this, again,
is just as well, for the peace of the world depends on a respect
for differences.

V. S. Pritchett in 1964

I think that I fell in love with Canada when the King and I came here in 1939. And each time I come back my feeling of affection seems to grow.

Lady Elizabeth Bowes-Lyon, mother of
Elizabeth II, in 1965

❋

Those scarlet-coated men quickly brought law and order to the wilderness ... For everyday duty the Mountie now wears a brown jacket, blue trousers, black shoes, and a forage cap. But the glamour remains. The Mountie is the image of Canada, the only policeman in the world who stands as the symbol of his country.

U.S. writer **Ralph Gray** in 1967

❋

Our spirituals ... were often codes. We sang of "heaven" that awaited us, and the slave masters listened in innocence, not realizing that ... heaven was the word for Canada and the Negro sang of the hope that his escape on the underground railroad would carry him there. One of our spirituals, "Follow that Drinking Gourd," in its disguised lyrics, contained directions for escape. The gourd was the Big Dipper and the North Star to which its handle pointed gave the celestial map that directed flight to the Canadian border.

U.S. civil-rights leader **Martin Luther King, Jr.**
in 1967

Of all the middle powers, Canada has the greatest resources, the most central position, the finest web of contacts and influences and, relatively speaking, the highest proportion of experts, both bilingual and in each language, of any nation in the world … A Canada prepared to pioneer with lucidity and daring the role of the first "international nation" in history would not only have an immense impact on its fellow states. It might also transform its own political life.

> British economist and population expert
> **Barbara Ward** in 1968

❋

Canada was the idealist's end of Empire—a people united in reconciliation, a colony emancipated, a wilderness civilized, the principles of parliamentary democracy transferred in triumphant vindication from an ancient capital to a new.

> **Jan Morris** in 1968

❋

I suspect, however, that the young men of deep sensitivity who have gone to Sweden or Canada or sought conscientious objector status or have willingly undergone jail sentences, would be the same men who, thirty years ago, memorized eye charts and travelled to Canada to enlist in Canadian forces rather than wait for American involvement in the war against Nazi Germany.

> Rep. **Paul N. McCloskey Jr.** (R-Calif.) in a 1971
> Congressional address, noting that Canada
> entered both World Wars before the U.S. The
> American pilot John Gillespie Magee, author
> of the war poem "High Flight," was killed
> in action with the Royal Canadian Air
> Force in 1941.

You have a conservative tradition as well as a liberal tradition, and these supplement and complete and sustain each other. The United States lacks and has suffered for the absence of what could be called a conservative tradition. The people we call conservatives are really nothing more than rich anarchists.

U.S. Senator **Daniel Patrick Moynihan** (D-N.Y.)
in a 1972 Toronto speech

✦

I like Canadians. As an ex-civil servant I hold your country in very high regard. You have the finest civil service in the world today. It was based on ours, I know, but it has surpassed it considerably. I suspect most Canadians don't realize it, but it is a fact recognized by civil servants everywhere in the world.

British novelist **C. P. Snow** in 1975

✦

About the political problems here I know little but I hope Quebec doesn't separate, with each province having its own language and culture. A country is better off when it's united as we are at home, where the South and North are stronger by virtue of being together.

U.S. playwright **Tennessee Williams** in 1977

✦

The world is greatly indebted to Canada for the patient, skillful and unassuming work of her statesmen in many international contexts, including the United Nations. Few countries can have attracted more genuine admiration, respect and liking, for their contribution to international affairs.

Anglo–Irish diplomat **Conor Cruise O'Brien** in 1978

Even the humble and inconspicuous Pilgrim Fathers enjoyed more publicity in England than all Canada and L'Acadie obtained in France. This helps to explain the bitterness of French–Canadian nationalists toward Mother France, who neglected their ancestors when they were few, poor and needy, and "abandoned" them to the English after they had formed a viable society. The third Republic honoured (?) Champlain by naming a second-class cruiser after him in 1874, and a store ship in 1919.

American historian **Samuel Eliot Morison** in 1972.
Of the French explorer and founder of New France, Morison writes: "No other European colony in America is so much the lengthened shadow of one man as Canada is of the valiant, wise and virtuous Samuel de Champlain."

♣

Canada is probably the most free country in the world, the only country with American possibilities, but few American problems, where a man still has room to breathe, to spread out, to move forward, to move out, an open country with an open frontier … Canada has created harmony and cooperation among ethnic groups, and it must take this experience to the world because there is yet to be such an example of harmony and cooperation among ethnic groups.

Ukrainian dissident **Valentyn Moroz** in 1979

♣

Canada has a role and ability to examine all world situations and to see the weak spots on all sides.

New York Times correspondent
Harrison Salisbury in 1980

Time and again in striving to improve consumer rights in the United States, my colleagues and I would make reference to a superior situation in Canada such as the provincial ombudsmen, cheaper pharmaceutical prices, complete health-insurance coverage, and greater concern over acid rain. The credibility in the United States of a reference to Canada is higher than an analogy to any other country because of the belief that Canada is on the same democratic wavelength.

> Consumer-rights advocate **Ralph Nader** in
> *Canada Firsts: Ralph Nader's Salute to*
> *Canada and Canadian Achievements*, 1992

❀

A new era is needed, one that beckons new levels of self-confidence to protect what Canada has that is best, which will benefit the U.S., too ... Such a benefit came home to me right after the publication of my book *Unsafe At Any Speed* in 1965. At that time, the U.S. news media were quite reluctant to report criticisms of cars by make and model, which the book did. It was difficult to interest television stations or networks in the issue of unsafe motor vehicles, or in my book. However, CBC's program "This Hour Has Seven Days" was interested, and I made my North American television debut in Toronto with the program beamed into autoland (Detroit) from the [CBC's] Windsor station. The U.S. media then followed with extensive coverage. Even before the Canadian program, the first documentary on unsafely designed automobiles was authored by the National Film Board [of Canada] whose producers had consulted and interviewed me in some detail.

> **Ralph Nader** in 1992

Democracy is so new to those of us who live in a South American country, where governments are self-chosen and there is no opposition. I love Argentina, but it's a bleak and hopeless country ruled by an irresponsible, incompetent and unethical government. But ah, Canada, here there is freedom.

> Argentine author **Jorge Luis Borges** in 1983,
> impressions of the House of Commons
> in session

❦

It is perfectly symbolic of Canada's historic predicament that anyone, especially English-speaking Canadians, thought they should have anybody's anything. What's the matter with a Canadian culture, Canadian efficiency, and Canadian government consisting of pieces from all over assembled into unique forms?

> **Andrew H. Malcolm** in 1985

❦

Here is a neighbouring country with tremendous economic, social and cultural similarities to the United States. Yet when I talk to Canadian trade unionists, or activists from the New Democratic Party, I realize that ideas that are prophetic, marginal or both in the United States are commonplace in the mass democratic Left just north of our border. In short, I feel our national inferiority on many policy issues, not its superiority.

> American socialist **Michael Harrington** in his 1987
> book, *The New Left: The History of a Future*

Canada is one of the few countries that does not have some rapacious animal as its national animal. It has a constructive animal, the beaver, which will not even bite your finger unless it is backed into a corner. And practically every other national flag has its origins in battle, while the Canadian flag is the maple leaf. It almost symbolizes a pastoral idyll.

Tom Wolfe in 1987

❖

The Soviet Union is bigger, but Canada is emptier, lonelier, lovelier, wilder, colder, leaner, cleaner, safer, duller, freer, saner, soberer, sweeter, neater.

U.S. travel writer **William Oscar Johnson** in 1988

❖

I came early to the belief that every incident in Quebec's struggle for recognition of its distinct language and culture would one day be repeated in the southern United States, with Spanish in our country replacing the role of French in Canada. Canada thus became of vital interest, and I followed with a microscope the twists and turns of how this nation of two languages sought to apply intelligent answers to the problem.

American novelist **James A. Michener**, discussing the origins of *Journey*, his 1988 novel set in the Canadian North

❖

It's too late for me to become Canadian, but I can understand the urge to be a Canadian.

British novelist **Anthony Burgess** in 1988

It is the expectation of Canada's social system to look after the people who cannot take care of themselves. There is no such expectation in the United States. That is a huge difference between our two countries. And if our two countries were conceivably one day to merge, I do not think that Canada's social welfare system would prevail in the United States.

U.S. novelist **John Irving** in 1990

❦

Canada is especially interesting to Americans because for years its health system was similar to theirs. But since it switched to national health insurance in 1971, it has managed the double feat of containing costs and looking after all its people.

Britain's **Economist** in 1991

❦

At a time when some 33 million Americans lack insurance, the Canadian health care system serves as a taunting reminder that with a few compromises it is possible to provide quality care for everyone, and for less money. In Canada there are few machines to blast apart kidney stones, but no women go without prenatal care. There is no Mayo Clinic, but there are also no emergency rooms teeming with people who cannot afford a family doctor.

New York Times report in 1991

If the universal coverage and single-payer features of the Canadian system were applied in the United States, the savings in administrative costs alone would be more than enough to finance insurance coverage for the millions of Americans who are currently uninsured.

> Report of the **General Accounting Office**, a nonpartisan auditing and investigative arm of the U.S. Congress, in 1991

❦

Canadians average 56 per cent more doctor visits for evaluation and management, and 20 per cent more surgical procedures than Americans ... Canadians receive less of only a handful of elective high-technology services, like coronary bypass surgery, which is clearly overused in the United States. As our General Accounting Office has documented, there are virtually no waiting lists for emergency surgery in Canada. A fair evaluation would state that Americans are more likely to die from unneeded surgery than Canadians to die while on a waiting list ... Canada's abundance of well-trained family doctors allows specialists to focus on their areas of expertise. In contrast, the United States suffers a shortage of primary care practitioners and a glut of underused specialists tempted to fill their calendars with unneeded procedures or patients outside their area of competence.

> **David U. Himmelstein**, M.D. and **Steffie Woolhandler**, M.D., associate professor and assistant professor, respectively, at Harvard Medical School, writing in *The New York Times* in 1992

An improbable country from the outset, Canada has always beaten the odds. In the eighteenth century, it chose dependence on faraway England over a merger with the thirteen colonies next door—and flourished as the largest dominion of the British Empire. In the nineteenth and twentieth centuries, it avoided much of the social and economic strife that troubled its neighbour to the south and gradually built an egalitarian society where poverty was nearly invisible, health care universal, higher education within everyone's reach, and civility at a level perhaps unique in the Americas.

Time in 1991

✦

With a parliamentary system like Canada's, the United States could have dealt with Watergate two months after it was discovered.

Richard Strout, columnist in *The New Republic*

✦

The most visible product of our current "gridlock" is the federal deficit. Canada has a deficit too—but it also has a system in which the prime minister controls the legislature. So how is Canada doing? It cut its deficit from 8.7 per cent of GDP in 1984-85 to 5.1 per cent in 1991–92. Meanwhile, the United States succeeded in cutting its deficit from 5.6 per cent of GDP to ... well, to 5.8 per cent.

Columnist **Mickey Kaus** in *The New Republic*,
in 1994

✦

There are very few countries that have provided troops as readily, as freely and as courageously as Canada.

British Prime Minister **John Major** in 1995, on the
role of Canadian peacekeepers in the Bosnia crisis

In a world darkened by ethnic conflicts that tear nations apart, Canada stands as a model of how people of different cultures can live and work together in peace, prosperity and mutual respect.

Bill Clinton in a 1995 House of
Commons address

✦

Canada has been a wonderful partner for the United States, and an incredibly important and constructive citizen throughout the entire world … I have seen how the leadership of Canada in so many ways throughout the world works, and what it means for the rest of the world to think there is a country like Canada where things basically work.

Bill Clinton on October 25, 1995, five days
before the Quebec sovereignty vote, breaking
with traditional diplomatic practice of avoiding
comment on the Canadian unity debate

✦

What is truly amazing is the voter turnout and the rallies that were held in Canada's other six provinces beseeching Quebec to vote "no." This display of national pride, and the outpouring of love toward their countrymen extols Canada and Canadians. As Americans, we should learn from this example.

Chelsea Clinton, 15, daughter of Bill and Hillary
Clinton, writing in a November 1995 edition of
the student newspaper at Washington, D.C.'s
Sidwell Friends School on the 90 per cent-plus
voter turnout in the recent Quebec referendum
on independence, in which she correctly
gauged the spirit of the occasion, if not the
precise number of Canadian provinces

For people outside Canada, including the investors who hold about 40 per cent of its public debt, it's hard to figure why anyone would want to break up such a nice country.

The Wall Street Journal in 1995

❦

Many [Quebecois], with their numbers dwindling and their French-based culture under attack, as they see it, from the cheerful consumerism of English-speaking North America, have turned to a nineteenth-century remedy—nationalism. Undoubtedly, with their long history, their language, their ties of blood, and the conservative Catholicism that still shapes their thinking, [French Canadians] are a true nation, in a sense that Garibaldi—or Theodor Herzl, for that matter—would have understood. Canada, by contrast, is a nation in the late-twentieth-century style: people of many backgrounds who share the same land and the same principles, and try to benefit from many cultures and creeds, in equality and mutual toleration. With lavish resources, English-speaking Canada —like Australia or the United States, or even Britain, modestly endowed though it is—has no trouble attracting immigrants, yet this is something that a nation based on blood and language can't do. The whole English-speaking world now accepts the new principles, at least in principle; but Quebec does not belong to the English-speaking world … The survival of the French of North America, and of their French, is important to us all, and is, indeed, in line with the goal of benefiting many cultures. The French Canadians have been the bravest of partners in the shaping of this continent, and of Canada in particular. To acknowledge as much is only historical justice.

Essayist **Murray Sayle** in *The New Yorker*
in 1995

Canada is one of the planet's most comfortable, and caring, societies. In 1992 and again last year, the United Nations Human Development Index cited the country as the most desirable place in the world to live. This year a World Bank study named Canada the globe's second wealthiest society after Australia, using calculations that weighed resources and investment in education and other social programs ... Widely hailed around the world, [Canada's universal and comprehensive health-care system] produces definite results: Canadian men and women live 1.5 years longer on average than their U.S. neighbours; infant mortality is also comparably lower; and Canada still manages to spend only 9.7 per cent of GDP on health care, vs. 14.2 per cent south of the border.

Time in 1995

✦

You Canadians have given us such hope to carry on. We admire your bravery ... You are the neighbour of such a rich, powerful country, and yet, you don't mind clashing with them. Well, that gives us more confidence.

Havana university math teacher and former diplomat **Pedro Gutierrez** in 1996, on Canada's defiant objections to the 35-year-old U.S. trade embargo on Cuba

A FUTURE OF GOOD FORTUNE

This will some time hence be a vast empire, the seat of power and learning. Nature has refused them nothing, and there will grow a people ... that will fill this vast space.

> British general **James Wolfe** on New
> France, just before his successful 1759
> engagement with Louis Montcalm on
> the Plains of Abraham

❖

Canada has held, and always will retain, a foremost place in my remembrace. Few Englishmen are prepared to find it what it is. Advancing quietly; old differences settling down, and being fast forgotten; public feeling and private enterprise alike in a sound and wholesome state; nothing of flush or fever in its system, but health and vigour throbbing in its steady pulse: it is full of hope and promise.

> **Charles Dickens** in 1842

I am not one of those who believe that the destiny of Canada must inevitably be annexation with the U.S. Canada possesses all the elements of a great independent country. It is destined, I sometimes say to myself, to become the Russia of the New World.

British prime minister **Benjamin Disraeli**

*

Her future can scarcely fail to be a noble one, for she carries within herself all the elements of healthy and beneficient prosperity. Her people are a brave, hard-working, simply-living folk, contact with whom freshens up and braces the spirit of the wanderer from the old world, as the superb climate does his body. Her soil teems with wealth for the worker, coal, iron, sulphates, oils, copper; her vast forests are of the finest timber; the motive power lying almost unused in her inland waters, is probably the cheapest and best in the world. Plenty and comfort are in all her borders, and nowhere (as yet at any rate) are there signs of the corruption and feebleness, which cling and festered round the huge accumulations of material wealth, raising problems which weigh so heavily on the brain, if they do not daunt the heart, of the bravest and truest men in older lands ...

Thomas Hughes in 1871

*

Canada still walks in unconscious beauty among her golden woods, and by the margin of her trackless streams, catching but broken glances of her radiant majesty, as mirrored on their surface, and scarcely recks as yet of the glories awaiting her in the Olympus of Nations.

Lord Dufferin, address in Belfast on embarking for governor-general duties in Canada, in 1872

It is only a question of time before you, the people of Canada, become, because of your numbers, if you remain united, high-souled, public-spirited and incorruptible, the most powerful factor, not only in the British Empire, but in the English-speaking world.

Governor-General **Earl Grey** in 1904

✿

Canada, the Scotland of America, is to play the part of Scotland and annex her southern neighbour as Scotland did, and boss it for good, both in Church and state, as Scotland also did— I need not speak here in the past tense—as she still does. Canada would take her somewhat strenuous, perhaps one might say obstreperous, brother by one hand and her mother by the other, put the one in the other and re-unite them.

Lord Carnarvon in a 1906 Ottawa address

✿

Does any one remember that joyful strong confidence after the war, when it seemed that, at last, South Africa was to be developed—when men laid out railways, and gave orders for engines, and fresh rolling-stock, and labour, and believed gloriously in the future? It is true the hope was murdered afterward, but—multiply that good hour by a thousand, and you will have some idea of how it feels to be in Canada—a place which even an "Imperial" Government cannot kill.

Rudyard Kipling in 1908

✿

God has made Canada one of those nations which cannot be conquered and cannot be destroyed, except by itself.

Norman Angell in 1913

The future of Canada, whether from the standpoint of civilization or from the viewpoint of the virtues of the kingdom, is very great. Day by day civilization and freedom shall increase. Likewise the cloud of the Kingdom will water the seeds of guidance in that Dominion.

Abdu'l-Baha, eldest son of Baha'u'llah, prophet
and founder of the Baha'i Faith. Abdu'l-Baha
visited Montreal in 1912

❋

Canada is going to be a wonderful country. There are many reasons why I should like to live for one hundred years. One of the reasons is I would like to see this country one hundred years from now. It will be great. It will be rich ... it will be powerful.

British statesman **Ramsey MacDonald** in 1928

❋

In the distance I seem to catch a glimpse of a great nation of fifty million people, ideally located, who through its strength enjoy peace and security. This great Nation, joined by close ties of blood and battle to the Old World and the New World, seems to me to form a hinge between the two.

Field Marshall **Bernard Montgomery** in a 1946
Canadian radio broadcast

❋

Canada is a place of infinite promise. We like the people, and if one ever had to emigrate, this would be the destination, not the U.S.A. The hills, lakes and forests make it a place of peace and repose of the mind, such as one never finds in the U.S.A.

English economist **John Maynard Keynes** in 1944

My friend Moline ... said, "What makes poetry is white paper." ... I cannot help but think that the same gift of white paper which is given to poets was given also to Canada by the Creator. Canada is a country with big white paper of tremendous possibilities, and I think it is what is most inspiring in your beautiful country. It is not only to think of the past, which is so glorious, and the present, which is so grand and impressive, but also of the future, which is so full of inspiration. I think that Canada is only at the beginning of its glorious and splendid career.

> French poet and diplomat **Paul Claudel** in 1928

❀

May I indulge in a generality and say with conviction that Canada being a young country is full of possibilities that are incalculable. She has neither exhausted her material resources nor those of her mind and character. She has not yet produced in her psychology the self-toxin of fatigue that old civilizations suffer from in the shape of cynicism and spiritual insensitiveness. Her creative youth is still before her ... Canada is too young to fall a victim to the malady of disillusionment and scepticism.

> Bengali poet and philosopher **Rabindranath Tagore** in a 1929 Victoria speech

❀

Canada is like an expanding flower; wherever you look you see some fresh petal unrolling.

> **Arthur Conan Doyle**, in his 1924 memoir, *Memories and Adventures*

222 CANADA INSIDE OUT

There are no limits to the majestic future which lies before the mighty expanse of Canada with its virile, aspiring, cultured and generous-hearted people.

Winston Churchill in a 1951 London, England address

＊

[Canada's identity], it must be admitted, is an obsession more noticeable on campuses and in CBC television and radio studios than in the marketplace. Listening to talk and speculation about it, as all must who frequent culturally conscious Canadian circles, I reflect inwardly that he who would keep his identity must lose it, and say over to myself an adaption of Blake's well-known lines: "Never seek to tell thy identity,/ Identity that never told should be,/For the gentle wind does move,/Silently, invisibly."

Malcolm Muggeridge in 1979

＊

It seemed to me that Canada, one of the world's best kept secrets, was an exciting place of new beginnings next door to an aging nation full of fear for its decay.

Andrew H. Malcolm, rationale for undertaking his 1985 book, *The Canadians*

＊

The world shares a sentimental approval of Canada— Mounties, biculturalism, slightly boring decency—which independence for Quebec would undermine. If tolerant Canada cannot share power across a linguistic divide, what hope is there for more bitterly riven societies?

Financial Times of London editorial in 1995

Canadian citizenship has its privileges indeed: despite the emotional push-and-pull over Quebec's status, the country is remarkably free of violent race, class or ethnic conflicts. It has one of the globe's best educated and healthiest populations, and blankets its legal residents with social subsidies. From the lush high-rise apartments abutting Vancouver's Stanley Park to the sleek bank towers of Toronto's Bay Street financial district, Canadian cities exude a sense of newly minted opportunity befitting a nation with a per capita income of $19,570 ... It is no coincidence that Canada attracts more immigrants yearly—217,000 in 1994—in relation to its population than all but a handful of countries.

Time in 1995

❖

When I'm in Canada, I feel this is what the world should be like.

U.S. actress **Jane Fonda**

INDEX